COUNTRIES OF THE WORLD

Chile

Gareth Stevens Publishing

A WORLD ALMANAC EDUCATION GROUP COMPANY

About the Author: A frequent traveler to Chile, Renée Russo Martinez has worked in marketing and public relations for more than ten years. She lives in the United States with her husband Rodrigo and their son Francisco.

PICTURE CREDITS
Jorge Acuña/International Bildarchive:
  35, 47 (top)
AFP: 14 (both), 29, 37, 60, 63, 75, 76,
  77, 78, 79, 82, 83, 84, 85
Art Directors & TRIP Photo Library:
  3 (center), 54 (bottom), 57, 89
Victor Engelbert: 40, 72, 74
Focus Team — Italy: 6, 43, 48 (bottom), 55
Getty Images/Hulton Archive: 62, 80, 81
Eduardo Gil: 1, 12, 15 (top), 23, 33
  (bottom), 48 (top), 50, 61, 68, 69
HBL Network Photo Agency: 38
Horst von Irmer/International Bildarchive: 2,
  3 (top), 4, 7, 8, 11, 16, 18, 21, 22, 24, 25,
  27, 28, 30, 31 (both), 34, 36, 39, 41, 42,
  44, 45, 49, 56, 58, 66, 70, 87, 91
Hutchison Library: 9, 33, 47 (bottom)
Lonely Planet Images: 59
South America Pictures: 17, 53, 67
Ricardo Carrasco Stuparchi: 3 (bottom), 13,
  15 (bottom), 20, 26, 32, 54 (top), 65, 73
Sylvia Cordaiy Photo Library Ltd: cover
Topham Picturepoint: 52, 64, 71
Maureille Vautier: 5, 10, 19, 46, 51

Digital Scanning by Superskill Graphics Pte Ltd

Written by
RENEE RUSSO MARTINEZ

Edited by
LEONG WEN SHAN

Edited in the U.S. by
**GUS GEDATUS
BETSY RASMUSSEN**

Designed by
ROSIE FRANCIS

Picture research by
SUSAN JANE MANUEL

First published in North America in 2003 by
Gareth Stevens Publishing
A World Almanac Education Group Company
330 West Olive Street, Suite 100
Milwaukee, Wisconsin 53212 USA

Please visit our web site at
www.garethstevens.com
For a free color catalog describing
Gareth Stevens Publishing's list of high-quality
books and multimedia programs, call
1-800-542-2595 (USA) or 1-800-387-3178 (Canada)
Gareth Stevens Publishing fax: (414) 332-3567.

© **TIMES MEDIA PRIVATE LIMITED 2003**
Originated and designed by
Times Editions
An imprint of Times Media Private Limited
A member of the Times Publishing Group
Times Centre, 1 New Industrial Road
Singapore 536196
http://www.timesone.com.sg/te

Library of Congress Cataloging-in-Publication Data
Martinez, Renee Russo.
Chile/by Renee Martinez.
p. cm. — (Countries of the world)
Summary: Provides an overview of the geography, history, government, people, arts, food, and other aspects of life in Chile.
Includes bibliographical references and index.
ISBN 0–8368–2358–3 (lib. bdg.)
1. Chile—Juvenile literature. [1. Chile.] I. Title.
II. Countries of the world (Milwaukee, Wis.)
F3058.5.M29   2003
983—dc21   2002030477

Printed in Malaysia

Contents

4

AN OVERVIEW OF CHILE

Throughout history, Chile has relied on foreign powers for trade and political support: Spain during the colonial period; Britain during the nineteenth century; and the United States in the twentieth century.

After more than a decade of military rule under General Augusto Pinochet Ugarte in the late twentieth century, Chile has resumed its democratic status. At present, the government cares about the well-being of its people, and human rights groups have made inroads into enhancing the status of Chile's minority native Indian population. In addition, the country's educational system is a model for the rest of South America and a healthy economy attracts people from all over the world to work in Chile.

Opposite: **The church in Santiago is one of many structures that was built by Europeans during Spanish rule.**

Below: **These strange statues on Chile's Easter Island have attracted the attention of anthropologists around the world.**

THE FLAG OF CHILE

The flag of Chile was officially adopted on October 18, 1817. Composed of two horizontal strips, the colors blue and white share the upper portion of the flag while the lower part of the flag is red. The blue field forms a perfect square and in its center is a single, white star. This star represents the powers of the state. The colors used on the flag are also highly significant. Blue represents the clean Chilean sky, white represents the snow of the Andes Mountains, and red represents the blood that was shed by Chilean nationalists during the country's battles for independence.

Geography

Chile is located along South America's Pacific coast. Long and narrow, the country has 4,000 miles (6,436 kilometers) of coastline, but it is only 265 miles (426 km) wide at its widest point. Easter Island, Juan Fernández Islands, and thousands of other smaller Chilean islands lie west of the coast. The country covers an area of 292,182 square miles (756,751 square km) and shares a border with Argentina, Bolivia, and Peru.

Mountains, Valleys, and the Coast

Three distinct geographical features dominate Chile's landscape: the coastal ranges, the central valley, and the Andes Mountains.

The Andes Mountain range is the longest mountain range in the world. The Chilean Andes provide a natural border that separates the country from Bolivia and Argentina. Among the Chilean Andes is Nevado Ojos del Salado, the highest peak in Chile. At a height of 22,614 feet (6,893 meters), it is one of numerous extinct volcanoes that are found in the Chilean Andes.

EASTER ISLAND

Also known as Rapa Nui, Easter Island is located 2,300 miles (3,700 km) west of the Chilean coast. The island is home to a small, mixed population. In the past, however, Polynesians were the island's sole inhabitants, and they carved the giant stone statues, called *moai* (moh-AH-ee), that continue to fascinate modern scientists from around the world.
(A Closer Look, page 54)

THE ATACAMA DESERT

Situated in northern Chile, the Atacama Desert is abundant in minerals and also home to the world's oldest mummies.
(A Closer Look, page 46)

Left: **Chile's National Park Corporation manages the Torres del Paine National Park, which has lakes, glaciers, and mountain ranges. Climbers come to the park to scale the magnificent granite mountains that date back millions of years.**

Left: Chile's Atacama Desert is one of the world's driest places.

About 5 percent of the land in Chile is arable and all of it is located within the central valley. The depression of the central valley is a catchment area for sediments that flow from the Chilean Andes. As a result, the area is rich in minerals, such as nitrates, coal, and copper. Chile's capital city, Santiago, is located in the central valley.

The coastal ranges do not have mountains as high as those found in the Chilean Andes. The northern and central coastal ranges also have flatter summits. At the southern tip of Chile, the Strait of Magellan separates Tierra del Fuego from the rest of the mainland.

Rivers and Lakes

South of Santiago is the Lake District, a mountainous region of forests, farmlands, parks, and waters, such as Ranco Lake and Llanquihue Lake. The Lao River in the north is the longest river in Chile, flowing about 275 miles (442 km) before emptying into the Pacific Ocean. Parts of many rivers in the country's north are dry because of little rainfall. The Bío-Bío and other rivers in Chile's south and central regions, however, have a more constant flow because of more abundant rainfall.

CHILOÉ ISLAND

With a land area of 3,241 square miles (8,394 square km), Chiloé Island, or Isla Grande de Chiloé, is South America's second-largest island. Separated from the mainland by the Chacao Straits, Chiloé Island is a sunken extension of Chile's coastal range.

(A Closer Look, page 48)

Climate

Chile has radically diverse climates. Because the country lies south of the equator, winter occurs between late June and late September, and summer begins in late December and ends in late March.

To the north, where Chile borders Peru, is the arid Atacama Desert. Rainfall in this region is very rare. In the city of Arica, the annual precipitation for the past fifty-nine years has hovered around 0.002 inches (0.005 cm).

In central Chile, the climate is mild, although summers tend to be dry while winters are often rainy. This climate attracts many winegrowers, who establish vineyards in the central valley. The mean temperature in Santiago is 69 °F (21 °C) in summer and 48 °F (9 °C) in winter. Annual precipitation in the capital is about 14 inches (36 centimeters).

Chile's south is characterized by cold and humid weather. Here, the rainfall is even higher than that of central Chile. Some parts of southern Chile receive as much as 200 inches (508 cm) of rain each year. In addition, the region also experiences strong winds and frequent storms.

EL NIÑO AND LA NIÑA

Inhabitants near the Pacific Ocean have noticed that in certain years, the ocean is warmer than usual during winter. These unusual climatic changes are called El Niño and La Niña. El Niño occurs every three to five years, while La Niña occurs less often. Both are far-reaching and have effects in places as distant as the United States and Australia. In the winter of 1979, due to El Niño, storms and flooding occurred in the northeastern and southeastern parts of the United States.

Left: **Grapes harvested from vineyards in Chile's central valley are made into wines and exported.**

Plants and Animals

Chile has many plants and animals that are unfamiliar to other parts of the world. In the northern desert area, the lack of rainfall yields little vegetation. Shrubs, patchy grasslands, and hardy cacti, which require little water for growth, make up the major vegetation in the north. In central Chile, forests of southern beech, pine, and eucalyptus are widely distributed. The world's largest tree, the giant alerce, and Chile's national tree, the araucaria, can be found in the country's south. The giant alerce can live up to four thousand years.

Chile's wildlife is equally diverse. A rare species of deer, called the pudu, is among the great variety of animals found in the country. Other animals include the camel-like guanaco, the endangered vicuña, the puma, and the alpaca. Rodents, such as the viscacha and the chinchilla, are found near the Andes and are known for their soft fur. Along the coast are many kinds of marine animals, such as sea lions, otters, penguins, seals, and various fish and shellfish. In the south, the plants and animals are protected by a huge system of national parks. Chilean birdlife includes Andean condors, ostrichlike rheas, Andean gulls, giant coots, penguins, and three species of flamingos.

Above: **The alpaca is related to the camel and the llama. A hardy animal, the alpaca thrives on the high Andean plateau.**

ENDANGERED WILDLIFE

Hunting and the loss of natural habitat are two of the major threats to the survival of Chilean wildlife. Chilean animals, such as the southern pudu and the Andean condor, face an uncertain future if the Chilean government does not implement laws to protect them.
(A Closer Look, page 56)

History

The early indigenous peoples of Chile were the Araucanians, who inhabited Tierra del Fuego and Patagonia. In the late 1400s, the Incas from Peru conquered most of northern Chile, but the Araucanians defended southern Chile from a similar fate.

Conquest and Colonization

Portuguese navigator Ferdinand Magellan was the first known European to see Chile. On October 21, 1520, Magellan and his crew passed the southern strait of Chile, which is now known as the Strait of Magellan.

In 1535, Diego de Almagro led the first Spanish expedition to Chile. Unable to find gold there, he moved north into Peru. Pedro de Valdivia led the second expedition to Chile in 1540. This time, de Valdivia and his men stayed on and founded the capital city of

THE MAPUCHES

The Araucanians' valor inspired the Chileans to mythologize them as the country's first national heroes. In 1553, the Araucanians fought the Spanish in a bloody battle, where de Valdivia and most of his men were killed. Of the three Araucanian groups, the one that mounted the greatest resistance to the Spanish were the Mapuches. The word "Mapuche" means "people of the land."
(A Closer Look, page 60)

VALPARAÍSO

Pedro de Valdivia proclaimed Valparaíso's status as a port of call in 1542. The city soon became the center of shipping activities in the Pacific.
(A Closer Look, page 68)

Left: This sketch shows two Araucanians, the earliest indigenous inhabitants of Chile.

Santiagó, on February 12, 1541. De Valdivia became the first Spanish governor of Chile and founded the cities La Serena, Valparaíso, Valdivia, Villaricca, and Concepcíon. The Araucanians, however, refused to bow to the European invader and repeatedly destroyed the Spanish settlements. Nonetheless, colonial rule in Chile lasted for more than three centuries, during which northern and central Chile were part of the Viceroyalty of Peru.

The Struggle for Independence

In 1808, French emperor Napoleon Bonaparte conquered Spain. With the Spanish monarch's loss of power, the colonies began to revolt. In 1810, local aristocrats in Chile gathered in Santiago to propose a change in government. They declared independence on September 18, 1810, and the Spanish governor had to resign.

Among the Chilean leaders was José Miguel Carrera, who became the new head of government in 1811. Chileans, however, were divided over the new status of self-rule. Some supported Carrera, while others, led by Bernardo O'Higgins, challenged him. Internal conflicts allowed Spanish forces to win the Battle of Rancagua in 1814 and reassert their control in Chile. Both Carrera and O'Higgins escaped to Argentina, where O'Higgins joined forces with Argentine general José de San Martín. In 1817, O'Higgins and de San Martín led an army across the Andes into Chile and defeated the Spanish army. Chile's independence was restored on April 5, 1818.

BERNARDO O'HIGGINS

Bernardo O'Higgins was actively involved in the movement that brought about Chile's independence from Spain. Today, he is widely regarded as the founding father of Chile.

(A Closer Look, page 64)

Left: **Bernardo O'Higgins (*center*) was forced by local aristocrats to resign in 1823. O'Higgins then lived in exile in Peru.**

The First Century of Independence

Chilean independence was insecure during the early years of O'Higgins' leadership. The Chilean elite were deeply divided over their support for either O'Higgins or Carrera. In 1821, O'Higgins ordered Carrera's execution, and Carrera was beheaded. O'Higgins tried to reduce the political influence of members of Chile's elite. His popularity declined and he was forced to abdicate in 1823.

O'Higgins' departure was followed by a period of political struggle between the conservatives, the liberals, and the army. Between 1823 and 1830, as many as thirty changes in government occurred. In 1831, General Joaquín Prieto Vial became the new Chilean president. In effect, however, it was Diego Portales Palazeulos, a merchant, who held the power in ruling Chile. In 1833, Portales drafted a new constitution, which remained in effect until 1925. In that time, the country maintained a strong central government and steadily grew in prosperity as Chilean products found their way into foreign markets.

Chilean cities grew rapidly in the mid-nineteenth century. The improved infrastructure of cities such as Santiago and Valparaíso drew large numbers of rural Chileans, as well as migrants from other countries, into the country's urban centers.

The end of the nineteenth century was marked by a period of war and unrest. Aside from the War of the Pacific (1879–1883), in which Chile fought Bolivia and Peru, the Chilean army also spent three years defeating the Mapuches, who staged constant revolts. Chile was also plagued by a civil war in 1891, in which Chilean aristocrats and British merchants, who controlled Chile's nitrate mines, challenged the government's increasing control of the country's minerals.

The Twentieth Century

After a brief period of military rule (1924–1925), president Arturo Allesandri Palma, who had been elected and resigned, was reinstated, and another constitution was written. This new constitution was developed over the years to recognize labor rights, separate the church from the state, and establish a social welfare system for Chilean citizens.

For much of the twentieth century, the country remained a democracy. In 1970, however, Salvador Allende Gossens became Chile's first elected Marxist president. During this time, Chile's economy worsened, and drastic inflation and food shortages led to frequent strikes. On September 11, 1973, the Chilean military, led by General Augusto Pinochet, attacked the Presidential Palace and ousted Allende's government.

THE WAR OF THE PACIFIC

Chile defeated Bolivia and Peru in the War of the Pacific and gained control of the Atacama Desert and its rich mineral deposits. The naval victories of this war are celebrated every May 21.
(A Closer Look, page 70)

WORLD WAR II

During World War II, Chile sold minerals, metals, and war supplies to the Allied Forces. In 1943, Chile renounced diplomatic relations with Japan and Germany.

Left: **President Salvadore Allende, who had selected Pinochet as Chile's general major, was ousted by his appointee in a 1973 military coup.**

Military Rule (1973–1990)

After the 1973 coup, General Pinochet dissolved the Congress, suspended the constitution, and banned all political activities. He became the absolute dictator of Chile. Thousands of civilians who opposed this new rule were tortured or murdered by the army; others simply disappeared. From 1975 to 1985, the Roman Catholic Church, although officially neutral, became the primary refuge for Chileans who were persecuted by Pinochet's regime.

Although Pinochet's regime brutally ignored the human rights of its citizens, it turned the Chilean economy around. By adopting a free market economy, private companies flourished and trade barriers were lifted to encourage import and export.

The Return to Democracy

Beginning in 1980, Chileans approved a constitution that sought a return to democracy. The public then voted against Pinochet in 1988, and he was deposed. In 1990, the newly elected Chilean president, Patricio Aylwin Azocar, and his civilian government restored democracy to the country. General Pinochet, however, remained as commander of the army until 1998. The successive governments were able to lower or maintain inflation and unemployment rates.

Above: **Chilean President Ricardo Lagos Escobar (*left*) greets Mireya Garcia (*right*), vice president of the Group of Detained and Disappeared. This group is made up of members who had been detained and tortured by general Pinochet's regime. Other members also include families of people who had gone missing after being arrested during the military rule that began in 1973.**

Left: **Members of the media watch as police investigators and experts from the Medical Legal Institute search for the remains of prisoners who were missing since the regime of former Chilean dictator General Pinochet.**

Gabriela Mistral (1889–1957)

Gabriela Mistral is one of Chile's most distinguished educators and writers. Born Lucila Godoy y Alcayaga, Mistral taught in many cities, including Santiago, Temuco, and La Serena, from 1906 to 1922. Mistral's ideas about education earned her the respect of fellow educators. In her poetry, Mistral portrayed themes of faith, love, and death. She later joined the League of Nations and visited Mexico and Europe to reform their schools and libraries. After entering the Foreign Service in 1933, Mistral served as an honorary consul to countries such as Brazil, Spain, and the United States. In 1945, Mistral became the first Latin American woman to receive the Nobel Prize for Literature.

Gabriela Mistral

Claudio Arrau (1903–1991)

Claudio Arrau was a Chilean pianist who gained international fame for his execution of Romantic classics. Making his debut in 1914, he was awarded the prestigious Liszt Prize in 1919 and 1920. Arrau then went on to perform in Europe and the United States, gaining fans from different parts of the world. Upset by the political climate in Chile, the Chilean pianist renounced his citizenship in 1967 and became a U.S. citizen. Arrau did not, however, turn away from his homeland, and he performed in benefit concerts to aid groups such as Amnesty International, which polices human rights abuses in countries such as Chile. Arrau returned to Chile to a hero's welcome in 1984.

Augusto Pinochet Ugarte (1915 –)

Born in Valparaíso, Chile, in 1915, Pinochet became general commandante of Santiago in 1971. In the same year, he was appointed by President Allende as general major of the state. In 1973, after leading the military coup that overthrew Allende, Pinochet imposed a strict military rule, and his regime tortured and killed thousands of Chileans who opposed him. In October 1998, eight years after he stepped down as president of Chile, Pinochet was arrested in London on murder charges. Although he was a senator, Pinochet was denied impunity. The Chilean Supreme Court, however, found him unfit to stand trial due to frail health.

Augusto Pinochet Ugarte

Government and the Economy

In October 1988, Chileans voted against the military rule of General Augusto Pinochet, which had been in place since 1973. The following year, Chile had its first presidential election in fifteen years, and Patricio Aylwin Azocar was elected president.

Today, Chile is a democratic republic and its head of state, or president, is elected through a popular vote. After winning the election, the new president appoints ministers to serve in the Cabinet. These ministers assist the president during his or her six-year term in office. In March 2000, Ricardo Lagos Escobar was elected president of Chile.

The Legislative Branch

The National Congress, or the part of government which makes decisions about the country's laws, consists of a Chamber of Deputies and a Senate. The Chamber of Deputies has a total of

THE MILITARY

In Chile, men have to serve in the military for a period of two years. For women, military service is voluntary and performed in noncombat units.

Below: **The National Congress building, previously located in the capital city, is now a familiar sight in Valparaíso.**

16

Left: Chile's Supreme Court is headed by a president who is elected by members of the court.

120 members, all of whom are elected by voters. Of the forty-eight senators, thirty-eight are elected by voters, while the other ten are appointed by the Supreme Court, the Armed forces, and the president. Senators serve an eight-year term, while members in the Chamber of Deputies serve a four-year term. The Security Council, the Supreme court, and the Constitutional Tribunal also have input into legislative decision.

The Judiciary

The president appoints judges to the Supreme Court from a list provided by members of the court. These judges are selected upon approval by the Senate.

Administrative Regions

Chile is divided into thirteen administrative regions, each led by an administrator. These regions have a total of forty provinces. Each province is headed by a governor. The provinces are in turn divided into municipalities, each led by its own mayor.

Political Parties

The leading political parties in Chile are the Christian Democratic Party (CDP), the Coalition of Parties for Democracy (CPD), and the Socialist Party (PS). Chile's current president, Ricardo Lagos Escobar, is from the PS.

THE WOMEN OF CHILE

Chilean women won the right to vote in national elections in 1949. In 2002, President Lagos appointed Michelle Bachelet as Chile's Minister of Defense. Bachelet is the first woman to become the Minister of Defense in Chile. In recent years, Chilean women have begun playing a greater role in society, making their voices heard in political, economic, and social arenas.

(A Closer Look, page 72)

Above: **Tourism is steadily growing in Chile, especially in busy cities such as La Serena.**

Economy

Chile has a market economy, which means that the production and sale of goods and services are based on the consumers' demand for them. Previously, the government controlled a large part of industrial resources, such as copper mining. Today, private companies play a significant role in Chile's domestic products.

Trade and Industry

Chile's economy improved significantly after the abolishment of General Pinochet's military dictatorship. In 1993, Chile had a gross domestic product of forty billion dollars. The country's manufacturing sector has also increased in importance. Inflation declined and the unemployment rate fell to a new low in 1993, when Chile opened its doors to foreign investors. Tax-free trade zones in the northern and southern parts of Chile attract foreign firms to the country. Companies from the United States, Canada, and Mexico became major investors in the country's growing industries, which include mining, fishing and forestry.

ENVIRONMENTAL ISSUES

During the economic expansion that began in the 1970s, the state of the environment was overlooked. Now, Chile is facing a number of environmental issues.

(A Closer Look, page 58)

Chile's largest export market is the European Union (EU), followed by the United States, Japan, and Brazil. Exported goods include copper, fish, and chemical products. Major import partners are the United States, the EU, Argentina, and Brazil. Import goods consist of consumer products, industrial machinery, and chemicals.

Agriculture

Chile is the largest fruit exporter in the world. Fruit exports are grown in Chile as well as other parts of South America. Some of the fruits harvested in Chile include apples and grapes. About 40 percent of Chile's fruit exports go to the United States.

Aside from fruit, Chile also exports wheat, barley, oilseeds, lentils, and peas. Chile remains competitive in the agricultural export market because companies practice efficient production by using modern machinery.

Livestock, such as cattle and poultry, are also valuable exports. The Canada-Chile Free Trade Agreement (CCFTA), which came into effect in 1997, allows export of duty-free beef and poultry from Chile to Canada.

COPPER

Northern Chile's enormous wealth in minerals has attracted international mining companies to exploit it. Today, Chile is home to the largest open pit copper mine in the world. The extensive mining activities in Chile, however, have taken a toll on the environment.
(A Closer Look, page 50)

PROCHILE

The Export Promotion Bureau, which comes under the Ministry of Foreign Affairs, sets up trade commissions throughout the world. Called ProChile, these commissions promote Chilean companies and products to foreign firms, and also assist in the quality control and the shipping of exports.

Left: **Farmers harvest wheat, which will be processed at the mill.**

People and Lifestyle

Some 75 percent of Chileans are mestizos, or people of mixed European and American Indian ancestry. Europeans, who arrived in the nineteenth and twentieth centuries, make up approximately 20 percent of the Chilean population; they are mainly of Spanish, British, and German descent. Three percent of the population are of unmixed Indian ancestry, and the remaining 2 percent is a combination of other nationalities.

The population is generally divided along the lines of social class rather than ethnicity, although income level is related to ethnicity. Chileans in the upper class are mainly of European descent. The mestizos make up a large part of the middle class, while the native Indians and the less well-off mestizos make up the lower class.

The country's population is largely concentrated in central Chile, especially in the capital city. As much as three-quarters of Chileans live in central Chile because of its favorable climate and fertile soil. This includes native Indians who still live in or around the area where the Mapuche reservations of the 1880s were located. Today, improved infrastructure and greater social mobility allow Chileans to travel around Chile with greater ease.

Left: **A large Mapuche population is living in Temuco. Here, a group of Mapuche youths and their school teacher take a break between classes.**

Homes

The native Indians are generally the poorest within the Chilean community. Some of them still live in small thatched-roof houses with dirt floors. Many of these dwellings are found near the Bío-Bío river or in other provinces that have a relatively large Mapuche population. Other people within the lower-class population may live in makeshift houses that do not have running water or electricity, usually located in the slums.

The middle-class population resides in apartments or houses, but compared to the urban upper class, their homes are much more modest. The upper-class population lives in large and well-furnished houses, and they usually employ servants to look after the household. The middle class may hire part-time housekeepers to tend to their homes, but this is not always the case. Because of the wide income gap, it is common to find luxurious houses and broken-down shacks in different parts of the same city.

Above: The upper classes often live in houses that have sprawling gardens. A stark contrast exists between the homes of the upper class and the lower class in Chile. Basic necessities such as electricity may not be available to the poorer segments of the population, while the rich can afford to hire gardeners and nannies.

The Average Family

The life expectancy in Chile is about seventy-five years. With a current population of 15.3 million, Chile had a growth rate of less than 1.2 percent in 2001.

Above: **Middle-class couples tend to have smaller families, often with only two children.**

The family plays an important role in Chilean society, and many Chileans maintain close ties with extended families. The father is usually considered the head of the household, but gender roles are not strictly enforced. Newlyweds are expected to move out of their parents' homes and set up their own households even though the couples' children may come under the care of close or even distant relatives. Adult friends of parents and elder relatives are affectionately addressed as "aunt" or "uncle" by children.

Divorce

Chile is one of the few countries in the world that does not allow divorce. Civil marriages can be annulled, but the property rights of the separated couples cannot be addressed legally. The Roman Catholic Church in Chile is against divorce. In 1988, the Chamber of Deputies passed a divorce bill, and the Senate is now debating the issue of legalizing divorce. Opinion polls show that a majority of the population is in favor of divorce laws. Today, President Lagos has placed this issue high on his list of priorities.

At Work

Chile has a labor force of about 5.8 million, while the country's unemployment rate is at about 9 percent. The majority of the population is employed in the service sector, while 27 percent are working in the industrial sector. Most of the middle-class inhabitants in Chilean cities have jobs in business and industrial sectors, while the rural population is involved in agricultural work. About 14 percent of the Chilean population have farming-related jobs in the countryside.

Child labor is a serious humanitarian issue in Chile, where approximately 107,000 Chilean youths between the ages of twelve and nineteen are working informally. Most of them have stopped attending school, working more than forty hours each week. In some cases, these youths are the sole breadwinners in their household.

In Chile, educated women face drastic discrimination at work, with female graduates earning only 57 percent of what their male counterparts receive. For the uneducated population, women earn 87 percent as much as men.

SOCIAL WELFARE

Many government agencies participate in the country's social welfare system to provide pensions, disability benefits, and unemployment benefits to the affected population. The social welfare system is under the supervision of the Ministry of Labor and Social Welfare.

Below: Most of the fish caught and processed in Chile are exported to foreign markets. The fish factories are staffed by the country's lower-class population.

Education

Chilean students begin primary school at the age of six. For the first four years, subjects include Spanish, mathematics, history, geography, art, and music. Students are also required to attend physical education classes. In the next four years of primary school, students will learn English, biology, metal work, and a host of other optional classes such as French and painting. Aside from foreign languages, all lessons are taught in Spanish. The same is true for all levels of education in Chile.

Upon completing their primary school education, students move on to secondary school. The first two years involve general studies courses. In their third year, students choose between a vocational course and a social sciences or natural sciences course. Vocational studies teach students practical skills that are needed in the workforce. The five areas of study are technical, maritime, commerce, agricultural, and industrial. Outside the classrooms, secondary school students may take part in summer camps and sports and games. The duration of secondary school is four years.

BIBLE STUDY

While religious education is optional in Chilean schools, it is offered twice a week through primary school.

Left: Education in Chile does not merely confine itself to the classroom. Aside from sports, school children also go on field trips. This primary school teacher brings his class on an excursion.

Higher Education

After secondary school, Chilean students may choose to pursue higher education in public or private universities. Before 1980, Chile only had publicly-owned universities. Today, most universities, whether public or private, receive some public funding. While public universities select students through the national test, private universities have their own admissions requirements. Most institutions of higher learning in Chile are independent of the government, although newly-established schools must pass standards administered by the Ministry of Internal Affairs and the Ministry of Education.

The subjects taught at Chilean universities include natural sciences and mathematics, economics and business management, engineering, social sciences, and religion. Aside from academic facilities such as libraries and laboratories, the major universities in Chile also have sports facilities and recreational centers. The Universidad Católica in Valparaíso even has its own radio station, film storehouse, and television channel. Another well-known university is the University of Chile. Located in Santiago, the university opened in 1843 and is Chile's oldest university.

Above: **The Catholic University of Chile, run by the country's Roman Catholic Church, is located in Santiago.**

ASTRONOMY

Interest in astronomy, which is the study of the universe beyond Earth's atmosphere, is expanding in Chile. In the mid-1990s, the Pontificia Universidad Católica de Chile set up a Department of Astronomy and Astrophysics, where researchers have access to observatories owned by international institutes in northern Chile. Joint research and information exchange programs are also established with foreign universities.
(A Closer Look, page 44)

Religion

The Chilean constitution guarantees freedom of religion. As much as 89 percent of the Chilean population is Roman Catholic, while the remainder includes Protestants and Jews. A recent survey shows that 43 percent of Protestants are converts from other religions. As for Catholics, as many as 98 percent were born into the religion. Even though Protestants in Chile are a minority, their numbers are now growing steadily. Protestants in Chile include Methodists, Lutherans, and Baptists. Some of the native Indians in Chile still practice their ancestors' shamanistic faith, wherein spirits are believed to inhabit nature.

Roman Catholicism

Although not all Roman Catholics in Chile attend mass regularly or strictly follow its practices, most of them receive sacraments for important events such as birth, marriage, and death.

Introduced to Chile by the Spanish during the mid-1500s, Catholicsm's influence can be clearly detected in the country's art. Murals, paintings, and sculptures, especially those from earlier centuries, often use religious symbols and scenes.

Below: **The more active members of the Roman Catholic Church attend mass on a regular basis and take part in religious retreats.**

Chile's Catholic Church plays a strong role in the nation's education system and social reforms. The Church and the state, however, are separate entities. The Church also owns schools, universities, hospitals, and even a radio station.

Above: **President Lagos meets the cardinal of the Roman Catholic Church during his inauguration tour.**

Law on Religion

In the past, Chile's Roman Catholic Church enjoyed a different set of regulations from the country's other religions. It was given a "public right" status which did not require registration with the Ministry of Justice. This "public right" also ensured that the government could not remove the Church's designation as a religious foundation. Non-Catholic religions, however, had to register with the ministry as private nonprofit organizations to receive tax exemption and the right to collect funds.

A new law on religion was implemented in March 2000. With this law, all religions can obtain "public right" status. Non-Catholic chaplains are permitted to perform their services in public areas including military units, hospitals, and prisons.

Language and Literature

Spanish is the official language of Chile. It was adopted when the Spanish colonialists arrived in the 1500s. The Spanish of Chile is almost identical to the Spanish spoken in Spain, with the exception of some words that are borrowed from native Indian groups. More than 96 per cent of the population in Chile speak Spanish.

Minority groups speak a number of languages that are passed down from the country's native Indian tongues. About two hundred thousand Mapuches in Chile speak Mapudungun, a native language that survived Spanish rule. This language has many dialects that are intelligible to one another, such as Pehuenche, Moluche, and Picunche. About eighty-five thousand Mapuches are able to speak and write in Spanish.

The Aymara, who live in Chile, Peru, and Bolivia, speak Aymaran, a language that has twenty-six consonants and three vowels. Presently, about forty-eight thousand people in Chile speak Aymaran.

Left: **About 95 percent of Chileans above the age of fifteen can read and write. For younger Chileans, the country's aggressive education system ensures literacy.**

28

Literature

One of the first literary works about Chile was composed by a Spanish soldier named Alonso de Ercilla y Zuniga during Chile's colonial period. He was a poet born in Madrid, Spain. Zuniga's work is entitled *La Araucana*, an epic poem set among the Araucanians and their Spanish invaders.

In the nineteenth century, Chilean writer Alberto Blest Gana was considered one of the best novelists in Latin America. Blest's most famous work was *Martin Rivas* (1862), which portrayed the lives of the upper class.

In the twentieth century, Chilean novelists began to show more concern for social issues that plagued their country. Baldomero Lillo was one of the first Chilean writers to use literature to address such problems. In *Sub Terra* (1904), Lillo wrote moving narratives about the working conditions of coal miners during the early years of the century. In the 1970, novelist José Donoso wrote the introspective *The Obscene Bird of Night* in the voice of a failed writer. Donoso moved to Spain in the 1960s and 1970s. After returning to Chile in the 1980s, he became a strong critic of General Pinochet's regime.

In 1982, Chilean author Isabel Allende wrote *The House of the Spirits*, a novel set in South America, which was made into a film in 1994.

PABLO NERUDA

Pablo Neruda is perhaps the most renowned Chilean poet. In 1971, Neruda was awarded the Nobel Prize for Literature at the Royal Swedish Academy for Science in Stockholm, Sweden.

(A Closer Look, page 62)

Arts

Because Chile was a Spanish colony and a European trading center, Chilean art, music, and architecture have been heavily influenced by European styles. Cathedrals, such as the one in Linares, reflect the expansive Spanish colonial style in architecture, while buildings in Valdivia and Puerto Montt reflect strong German influences.

Art Museums

In the area of visual art, Chilean painter Pedro Lira Rencoret took the first step in promoting his fellow artists by founding a Chilean artists' union in 1885. Twenty-three years later, the union opened the doors to the nation's first art museum, the Museo Partenon. Located in the capital, the Museo Partenon was restored in 1945 and renamed the Contemporary Art Museum of Santiago. Other art museums in Chile include the National Museum of Fine Arts, which was built by the Chilean government in 1910.

Ancient and traditional Latin American artifacts, such as pre-Colombian art and folk art, are housed in Chile's Museo Chileno de Arte Precolombino and Museo de Arte Popular Americano.

Below: Chile's Contemporary Art Museum houses the works of Chile's finest artists. International exhibitions are also held in this museum.

HANDICRAFTS

Woven baskets, knitted and woven textiles, and ceramics are some of Chile's traditional handicrafts. In the city of Pomaire, the sale of handicrafts provides the main source of income for the local residents.

Celebrated Artists

Chile has a long tradition of artistic talents. One such artist was Nemesio Antunez, a muralist, printmaker, and painter who portrayed landscapes and figures as simple geometric shapes. A former director of Chile's Contemporary Art Museum as well as the National Museum of Fine Arts, Antunez's works have found their way to many international art galleries. His fellow artists include Chilean surrealist painter Roberto Matta, who went to Europe in 1933 to pursue his artistic career. Heavily influenced by Spanish artists such as Salvadore Dalí, Matta's works often used a bright palette to depict contorted human figures. Other artists include Isabel Klotz, who is known for using mixed media in her works, including paints and photographs, while Maria Angelica Mirauda practices engraving. Although early Chilean art focused largely on religion, the subjects that the current artists pursue are becoming more secular in nature. For instance, artist Mario Toral created a mural which portrayed scenes in a subway station, titled *Visual Memory of a Nation*.

Above: This sculpture of an eagle is made from lapis lazuli, a blue semi-precious stone found only in Chile and Afghanistan. The lapis lazuli is Chile's national stone.

Forging a Distinct Theatrical Tradition

Theater productions came into force in the early 1900s, when the country's universities began to show support for playwrights and theater companies. Founded in the 1930s by professors and students from the University of Chile, the Teatro Experimental was one of the first groups to perform distinctly Chilean dramas. Teatro Experimental founded theaters in various parts of Chile, including Antofagasta, Chillán, and Concepcíon, and led other theater companies in pursuing works that had social and political relevance. One renowned playwright was Armando Moock, who often portrayed the issues that faced the fast-growing urban middle class in Chile

When Pinochet's rule began in 1973, private theater groups were banned from performing plays that commented on Chile's political state. Only classical plays were allowed. However, these private theater groups changed the contexts and altered the lines in the classics in order to deliver their opinions on military rule.

Today, several theater festivals are held in Chile, such as the Political Theater Festival, which is an international collaboration that focuses on political issues. Acting workshops are also widely available for both amateurs and professionals.

TELEVISION

The number of theater audiences fell in the 1960s when television rose in popularity. The middle class in Chile ballooned as the nation's economy improved, and the more comfortable lifestyle led to a drop in audiences who were interested in plays that had a strong political or social slant.

CUECA — THE NATIONAL DANCE

A lively and energetic dance that is performed throughout the country, the *cueca* (KWHEY-kah) is the national dance of Chile.
(*A Closer Look, page 52*)

Left: Designed by French architects in the nineteenth century, the Municipal Theater in Santiago was opened in 1857. Today, the theater showcases some of the finest ballets, operas, and philharmonics to tour South America.

A FIRM PROTEST

Victor Jara openly sang the anthem of Allende's party, which he strongly supported, after his arrest in 1973. A few days later, his discarded body was found. The hands of the corpse had been broken. Many people believe that the police had broken Jara's hands to stop him from playing the guitar.

Music of the People

Chilean folk music is an important part of the oral traditional in the country. Folk songs often tell stories that relate to the history of the nation. These songs are usually accompanied by musical instruments, such as the cactus rainstick which can imitate the sound of rain. Other musical instruments include the *guitarron* (gee-tah-ROHN), a large bass guitar used by minstrels, and the *bombo* (BOHM-boh), a percussion instrument that goes back to pre-Colombian times.

Violeta Parra is a celebrated figure in Chilean folk music. A talented performer and composer, Parra reflected the lives of Chilean peasants and workers in her music. Her extensive tours throughout Europe brought the folk music of Chile to a wide audience. One of her Chilean fans was Victor Jara, who also became a folk singer. Jara went a step further by using his music to protest against the class division that was evident in Chilean society during the 1960s. A strong supporter of President Allende's Marxist government, Jara was shot to death after he was arrested and detained as a political prisoner by the new junta under Pinochet in 1973.

Above: **Violeta Parra was a prolific folk musician who gave audiences around the world an unforgettable taste of Chilean folk songs. Later in life, Parra took up weaving and made many beautiful Chilean handicrafts.**

Leisure and Festivals

Although Chile is now a modern nation, its citizens still enjoy some traditional pastimes, especially in the countryside. One such activity is kite-flying. Residents in Santiago go to the parks to fly their colorful kites on weekends during spring and summer. Parks are also favorite spots for picnics. One of the most popular parks in the capital, the Parque Metropolitano, has walking trails and also a zoo.

Aside from visiting the parks, Chileans also enjoy going to the beach. The sandy beaches in La Serena, Viña del Mar, and Villarrica are frequented by Chileans who go there to surf, play volleyball, or simply relax.

Chileans living in the city also enjoy going to shopping malls, sidewalk cafes, and restaurants. In the evenings, they may visit dance clubs or piano bars. The streets of Bellavista in Santiago have many pubs and dance bars that cater to the young residents who enjoy the nightlife. Many handicraft shops are open until late in the night, and Bellavista is a hive of activity even as night falls.

Left: **Santiago's Forest Park is a colorful sight as vendors sell their wares to families who come to relax during weekends.**

Above: **The game of chueca is still a popular sport among the native Indian population.**

Traditional Games

One of the traditional games played by Chileans is *rayuela* (rah-yoo-EH-lah). Originating in Spain, this game is commonly played by men of all ages. A player has to cast a heavy metal disc toward a suspended rope. The object of the game is to land the disc on the rope. A similar game is played by children, using coins instead of the heavy disc. Rayuela is also played in other countries, such as Argentina and Colombia.

The Mapuches play the traditional game of *chueca* (CHWEH-kah), which is somewhat similar to hockey. Chueca is played on foot, and each team has twenty players. Using curved wooden sticks and a wooden ball, players try to get the ball across their opposition's goal lines set at the opposite ends of the field. Chueca was forbidden during Spanish rule.

Children also play familiar games such as spinning tops, hoola hoops, and hopscotch. Using the metal hoops that secure wine barrels and wooden sticks, Chilean children roll the hoop along the ground, making sure that it does not fall on its side.

Sports

With its diverse geography and breathtaking landscape, Chile is perfect for outdoor activities. One traditional sport is horseback riding. From the early Araucanians to the present population, the horse has been an important part of life. Although widely used as beasts of burden in the countryside, horses are also the perfect mode of transportation. Chileans and tourists often enjoy the scenic views of Torres del Paine, the Atacama Desert, and Chiloé Island on horseback.

For risk-takers, the Chilean rodeo is a daring alternative to horseback riding. Every autumn for the past fifty years, a rodeo championship will be held where *huasos* (WAH-sohs), or Chilean cowboys, travel from village to village to compete. Unlike other rodeos, the huasos do not use any ropes when steering the cattle; instead, they ride on horses and try to guide cattle into a crescent-shaped barricade. During the competition, musicians strum on their guitars and perform popular folk songs while spectators cheer the huasos on. Huasos wear bright ponchos, wide-brimmed hats, and shiny boots with large spurs.

Above: **The Chilean rodeo is one of the most eagerly-anticipated sporting events in the country.**

CONVENTIONAL SPORTS

To enjoy the outdoors and keep fit at the same time, Chileans enjoy fishing, skiing, water-skiing, scuba-diving, and hiking.

Crowd Favorites

Like most countries in South America, *fútbol* (foot-BOL), or soccer, is one of the most popular spectator sports in Chile. The Santiago National Stadium was completed in 1962 for the FIFA World Cup, in which Chile came in third, after Czechoslovakia and Brazil. Ivan Zamorano is the current captain of Chile's soccer team. He led the Chilean team at the Sydney Olympic Games in 2000, when the team won the its first medal in Olympic soccer. Another rising football star is striker Marcelo Salas, who is known to fans as *El Matador*, or "the bullfighter."

Chile has also produced many fine athletes in other sports. Marathon runner Miguel Plaza Reyes won the Olympic silver medal in Amsterdam in 1928. Chilean swimmer Victor Contreras crossed the icy waters of the Strait of Magellan in the 1970s. In 2001, Chilean driver Eliseo Salazar took the fifth place in the prestigious Indy Racing League. Today, Marcelo Rios is one of the best tennis players to come from Chile. Born in Santiago, Rios has competed in the Wimbledon and the Australian Open, winning a total of eighteen singles titles to date.

Left: **Chilean soccer star Ivan Zamorano autographs the shirt of a young Chilean fan in Santiago.**

Festive Celebrations

A large number of the holidays celebrated in Chile are religious. Chileans may hold their own private celebrations on these days or participate in mass celebrations, involving the entire community.

Holy Week

Holy Week in Chile is also known as Semana Santa. It begins on Palm Sunday, which usually falls in late March or early April, and ends on Easter Sunday. During Holy Week, Chileans attend mass and remember the cruxificion and resurrection of Jesus Christ. After Holy Week is Cuasimodo, a Chilean religious festival that is celebrated throughout central Chile. This tradition began in the colonial period, when priests would visit people who were too sick to attend mass and receive sacrament on Easter Sunday. Back then, priests who made the trek to people's homes were protected from bandits by huasos. Today, although largely symbolic, huasos continue to accompany the priests on their rounds.

MUSIC FESTIVAL

The annual International Song Festival is held in Viña del Mar. Now in its forty-third year, the music festival has a competition in which any musician can participate. Many renowned bands such as The Black Crowes, Bon Jovi, and The Police, have graced the event.

Below: Brightly-adorned carriages, bicycles, and carts are part of the colorful Cuasimodo parade.

La Tirana

From July 12 to July 15, the village of La Tirana in the north of Santiago receives more than forty thousand visitors. They arrive at La Tirana to celebrate a festival of the same name. The story behind the festival is that of a native Indian woman. After the murder of her father by the Spanish, the woman would kill any Spaniard that came near her or her people. For this, she was known as *la tirana*, or "the tyrant." One night, she captured a Spanish miner, whom she fell in love with. Her people killed her when she converted to Catholicism. La Tirana became Chile's patron saint, the Virgin of Mount Carmel.

New Year's

On New Year's eve, families enjoy barbecues, or *asados* (ah-SAH-dohs). The traditional foods taken on New Year's Eve may include lentils, a spoonful of which is sometimes eaten for good luck. On this occasion, people may put money or travel tickets in their pockets to ensure the year ahead is filled with adventure and riches. Dazzling fireworks are displayed at the stroke of midnight to usher in the new year.

SEPTEMBER 11

Declared a holiday by General Pinochet to commemorate the day President Allende was removed from office, this holiday has since been abolished. Now changed to National Unity Day and celebrated on the first Monday of September, the holiday often marks a day of protests.

Food

Unlike the cuisines of neighboring countries, Chilean food is generally simple, consisting mainly of meat or seafood dishes. Nevertheless, the food is tasty and distinctive.

Seafood

Chile's long coastline provides an abundance of fresh seafood, including tuna, trout, hake, eel, lobster, and crab. Popular dishes include broth with fresh seafood and fish or shellfish marinated in lemon juice and served chilled. One other Chilean favorite is baked South American razor clams topped with melted Parmesan cheese. Many fish dishes are served with a thick sauce made of butter, bread crumbs, cheese, and spices. Chilean sea bass was once a local favorite but is now an international delicacy. Chile is also the second-largest producer of salmon, after Norway, and this fish is extremely popular either marinated or oven-baked.

Traditional Foods and Snacks

A common dish in Chile that is usually consumed during summer is *cazuela* (kah-SWEH-lah), a broth with rice, potato, and corn on the cob added. *Pastel de choclo* (pah-STEHL dee CHOH-klo) is a

Left: Chile's proximity to the coast means that seafood is a large part of a Chilean's diet. Chilean wine is a common beverage to accompany a hearty seafood meal.

Left: This store is selling freshly baked empanadas, a quick snack found not only in Chile but also in many other South American countries.

SWEET DESSERTS

Chileans enjoy rich sweet desserts. An amazing array of pastries include pastry stuffed with fruit and *alfajor* (ehl-fah-HOHR), which is layers of caramelized milk and thin pastry rolled in sugar. Other popular desserts include chilled rice with milk, sugar, and cinnamon, and flan topped with caramel.

popular corn casserole made from meat, vegetables, olives, and layers of mashed corn. "Poor man's steak" is a well-known beef dish, which is steak topped with fried egg and onions. *El completo* (ehl kohm-PLEH-toh), a hot dog topped with tomatoes, ketchup, mayonnaise, and guacamole, is possibly the most popular food in Chile.

Salads also make up an important part of Chilean cuisine. Salads consist of cold vegetables, topped with oil and lemon. Lettuce, however, is not always one of the ingredients. A well-known Chilean salad is *ensalada chilena* (ehn-sah-LAH-dah chee-LEH-nah), which consists of sliced tomatoes and onions, with oil, vinegar, and cilantro dressing.

A popular snack among Chileans is the *humita* (oo-MEE-tah). A humita is made by grating and mixing corn into a paste with fried onions, basil, salt, and pepper. The mixture is then wrapped in a corn husk and steamed. *Empanadas* (ehm-pa-NAH-dahs), or baked turnovers, are another favorite snack. A typical Chilean empanada is filled with a mixture of chopped beef, hard-boiled eggs, onion, olives, and raisins. Other fillings include cheese and seafood. Sandwiches made from steak or ham with cheese are also popular.

POPULAR BEVERAGES

Chileans enjoy a wide range of drinks on different occasions. Some of these beverages are consumed regularly as part of the Chilean diet, such as Chilean wine and *pisco* (PIS-koh), a brandy made from muscat grapes.

(A Closer Look, page 66)

A CLOSER LOOK AT CHILE

People and places make up Chile's unique identity. The minority native Indian population, consisting mainly of Mapuches, has retained much of their traditions in a fast-changing nation. With the help of several international foundations that look after the interests of this marginal group, the Mapuches are now able to voice their concerns to the Chilean government.

Historically, Chileans have always put up a fierce struggle for their country's autonomy. The nation's founding father, Bernardo O'Higgins, was a leader in this fight.

Opposite: **A cobbler prepares the shoe that goes on the traditional saddle used by huasos in the Chilean rodeo.**

Aside from the colorful cultures and personalities that hail from Chile, the country is also home to several important and exotic locations. The once vibrant port of Valparaíso brought numerous foreign traders to this narrow strip of land, while the mining of valuable minerals in the Atacama Desert continue to contribute to the wealth of the country. The clear skies of the Andes Mountains and the mysterious Easter Island have attracted astronomers and anthropologists around the world.

Above: **A mother and her son tour Easter Island on horseback. The exotic island attracts more than fifteen thousand tourists each year.**

Astronomy

Northern Chile is home to world-class astronomy facilities. With its clear skies and low humidity, this region's weather is ideal for astronomy. Many high-powered telescopes are located in this part of the country, and Chile has the most number of observatories south of the equator.

Astronomical Development

In the 1960s, several international scientific institutions came to the Southern Hemisphere to study the previously unexplored skies. International institutions, such as the European Southern Observatory (ESO) and Association of Universities for Research in Astronomy, Inc. (AURA), sent researchers to the region north of Santiago to find suitable sites. Soon, observatories were built at La Silla in the Andes, Cerro Tololo, and Las Campanas.

Below: Observatories in La Silla are managed by the ESO.

44

Left: Astronomers from the United States and other parts of the world study constellations above Earth's atmosphere in special laboratories located near the Andes.

Today, two of the world's most ambitious astronomy projects are under development in Chile's Atacama Desert: the Atacama Large Millimeter Array (ALMA) near Cerro Chajnantor and the Very Large Telescope (VLT) in Cerro Paranal. Both projects are being carried out by the ESO. The highly sensitive VLT will be able to capture images that are as far as 1.3 billion light-years away. This will allow astronomers to observe faraway galaxies that are hidden by thick curtains of dust particles and calculate the moment when the first light appeared in the universe.

Chilean Research and Brown Dwarfs

Since the mid-1990s, an agreement between the government and international observatories in Chile has guaranteed local astronomers regular access to these facilities. Ten percent of all observatory time is reserved for Chilean scientists. Such a measure has greatly increased Chilean astronomy research.

One of Chile's most renowned astronomers is Maria Teresa Ruiz. She has worked in several North American and European universities and is an astronomy lecturer in the University of Chile. In 1997, Ruiz became the first astronomer to receive Chile's Presidential Science Prize. That year, Ruiz discovered a brown dwarf, which is a star that does not generate heat or light, near our solar system.

LIGHT-YEARS

A light-year is a unit of length used in space measurements. One light-year is equivalent to the distance that light travels in a vacuum in one year, which is 5.88 trillion miles (9.46 trillion kilometers).

The Atacama Desert

Located predominantly in the Antofagasta and Atacama regions of northern Chile, the Atacama Desert stretches south 600 to 700 miles (965 to 1,126 km) from the Peruvian border. Flanked by the Andes Mountains to the east and coastal mountains to the west, the Atacama Desert is located next to the Pacific Ocean. Ocean currents keep clouds just off the coast so most rain falls into the nearby ocean. Although these currents bring fog to the desert, the desert receives little or no rain. As a result, the Atacama Desert is one of the driest deserts in the world.

A Disputed Region

Due to the area's rich source of minerals, notably sodium nitrate, the Atacama Desert was the center of various conflicts among Chile, Bolivia, and Peru throughout the nineteenth century. At this time, most of the area belonged to Bolivia and Peru, but the companies mining the deposits were Chilean. Conflict over the ownership of these minerals led to the War of the Pacific, from which Chile gained control of the entire area.

ATACAMA'S NATURAL WONDERS

Although immensely arid, the Atacama Desert boasts many amazing natural wonders, such as salt flats, oases, geysers, lagoons, and volcanoes. The desert's salt flats are home to different types of birdlife, including three species of flamingos. Valle de la Luna, or Valley of the Moon, is named for its unusual rock formations that resemble the Moon's surface. Located in the northern part of the desert are the El Tatio Geysers. At an elevation of about 14,000 feet (4,267 m), the El Tatio Geysers form the highest geyser field in the world.

Left: **One of the many natural attractions in the Atacama Desert is the El Tatio Geysers. A geyser is a hotspring that occasionally sends out jets of water.**

The Chinchorro and Their Mummies

The earliest known settlers in the Atacama Desert were the Chinchorro, a fishing community that lived along a stretch of the coastline running from southern Peru to Antofagasta in northern Chile. Scientists and archaeologists believe these people moved into the area more than nine thousand years ago.

Although little is known about the Chinchorro's daily life, the people are known to have practiced elaborate methods of preserving their dead. Scientists uncovered the first Chinchorro cemetery in 1983 and have since established that the Chinchorro mummies are the oldest mummies in the world. Around seven thousand years ago, the Chinchorro began producing what are now known as black mummies — bodies that were mummified and then painted with a layer of black manganese. This process changed over time, and red paint replaced black paint. A special feature of Chinchorro mummification was that this custom was not reserved for people of high rank or status; everyone was mummified regardless of gender, age, or social status. About two hundred and eighty-two Chinchorro mummies have been uncovered in the Atacama Desert.

Below: About 282 Chinchorro mummies have been uncovered. One hundred and forty-nine bodies were mummified by the Chinchorro, while the remaining bodies were naturally preserved in the arid sands of the Atacama Desert.

Chiloé Island

Chiloé Island is located off the coast of southern Chile. Stretching for 112 miles (180 km) from north to south, Chiloé Island is the second-largest island in South America, after Argentina's Tierra del Fuego.

The South Panamericana Highway, which extends from the town of Putre at the northern tip of Chile, links Chiloé Island to the mainland. On this highway route, the closest mainland town to Chiloé Island is Puerto Montt.

Coastal ranges on Chiloé Island divide the island lengthwise. Because of these mountains, the island has two distinct climatic environments. The side that faces the Pacific Ocean experiences stormy conditions, with heavy rain and strong winds. Sheltered by the mountains, the other side of Chiloé Island has much more pleasant weather.

Above: **Chiloé is Chile's land of myths. The local folklore is filled with stories of mythic creatures, such as La Pincoya (*below*), the goddess of fertility, and Trauco, an ugly forest dwarf who kills men and seduces women who wander into the woods.**

CHILOÉ ARCHIPELAGO

The Chiloé archipelago is located in the waters between the eastern shoreline of Chiloé Island and the western border of mainland Chile. Some of the thirty-three islands within the Chiloé archipelago are so close to one another that it is possible to walk from one island to the next when the tide is low.

Left: **Colorful fishing boats dock at the island's coast. Fishing is a common livelihood for the coastal community.**

Before the Spanish settled on Chiloé Island in 1567, the only inhabitants on the island were native Indians, who tended to be either Mapuches-Huilliches, Chonos, or Caucahues. Following Spanish occupation, Chiloé Island was cut off from the Chilean mainland for more than 250 years. The last of the Spanish forces left the island in 1826, after their defeat in Ancud, a town at the northern tip of Chiloé Island.

Today, a large part of the island's population is of mixed Spanish and native Indian ancestry. Most of the inhabitants are devout Catholics. Their way of life is well adapted to the maritime environment, with many houses built on stilts high above the water. Local handicrafts include various wooden or stone artifacts and high-quality, hand-loomed wool textiles.

Churches of Chiloé

Chiloé Island has 150 churches, which are magnificent structures that combine European architectural styles with indigenous building techniques. Many of these churches are made of wood, and eight of them are listed as Chilean national monuments. The church in the town of Achao has been marked by the United Nations Educational, Scientific and Cultural organization (UNESCO) as a heritage building. After years of neglect and decay, the island's churches are now being restored.

Copper

About 30 percent of the world's copper reserves are located in Chile, the world's largest producer of copper. Northern Chile is home to some of the world's largest copper mines, including Escondida and Chuquicamata. Forty percent of the world's annual copper production takes place in Chile. In 2000, Chile produced 4.5 million tons (4.1 million metric tonnes) of copper.

Economic Bonus

The Chilean economy has relied heavily on copper production for nearly two hundred years. In the early nineteenth century, Chile's vast copper reserves attracted a large number of British and American foreign investors. In 1835, the foreign companies exported as much as 12,700 tons (11,521 metric tonnes) of copper, which were sold mainly to the United States.

For more than a century, Chile's copper industry had been controlled by foreign mining companies. In 1951, an agreement

Below: The production of copper dominated the Chilean economy from as early as 1860, when the copper exported accounted for 55 percent of the country's trade. Since so much of Chile's resources are focused on one industry, the Chilean economy is always at risk of crashing should the price of copper fall drastically, as it did in 1991.

signed in Washington gave the Chilean government 20 percent of the annual amount of copper produced in the country. From the 1950s to the 1960s, the Chilean government increased its control over the country's copper industry by implementing new laws. By 1971, the Chilean government had declared that the assets of all foreign companies that were involved in copper production were to become state property. Established in 1976, state-owned National Copper Corporation of Chile, or Codelco Chile, enjoyed a monopoly over the country's copper industry until the early 1990s. Today, multinational mining giant BHP Biliton owns 57.5 percent of Escondida, the largest copper mine in Chile.

An Environmental Hazard

In the early 1990s, local farmers and fishermen in the Port Caldera region launched a combined lawsuit against Codelco for seriously damaging the environment. The company's operations in the area had been releasing large amounts of carbon monoxide and arsenic into the air and water sources. The furnaces at Chuquicamata, formerly Chile's largest mine, were closed for the month of July in 1994 to comply with environmental regulations.

Cueca — The National Dance

A lively, fast-paced dance, the cueca is the national dance of Chile. Although the dance has been performed since the days of Spanish colonialism, it did not become the national dance until 1979.

The origins of the dance are uncertain. Some believe that the dance is of African or Indian origin, while others argue that the roots of the dance are distinctly European. Traditionally, the cueca was performed in the Chilean countryside before its popularity spread throughout the country.

A Vigorous Dance

The cueca is essentially a courtship dance that is performed by a couple. The dance begins with the man approaching the woman and offering his arm. The woman rises and accompanies him on a brief stroll. They then face one another, each with a handkerchief in hand, and begin to dance. The first steps are very calculated and calm. The couple dance separately but never lose eye contact.

Left: **When performing the cueca, the man's steps imitate the rooster's amorous struggle, while the woman follows the defensive and cautious nature of the hen.**

The couple wave the handkerchiefs as they dance around each other. As the dance progresses, the steps of the male dancer become more and more complicated as he picks up speed. The dance ends when the man, with one knee on the ground, places his arm around his partner. The movements of the dance have been likened to the courtship ritual between a rooster and a hen.

The performers dance to the musical accompaniment of singing and instruments such as the guitarron, accordion, and harp. Hand-clapping and loud cheers from the audience add to the excitement of the dance and encourage the dancers. Although the dance steps differ from region to region, Chileans regard the cueca as a celebratory dance that is performed at special occasions, such as national holidays.

A Protest Dance

A distinct version of the cueca has emerged in recent years. As a form of protest against the military government of the 1970s and 1980s, Chilean women perform the cueca without partners and sometimes with photos pinned to their clothing to highlight the disappearance of their loved ones during General Pinochet's rule.

Easter Island

One of the world's most remote inhabited islands, Easter Island, is located in the eastern Pacific Ocean, 2,300 miles (3,700 km) west of Chile. Named Easter Island by the Dutch, who were the first Europeans to discover the island in 1722, the island has been a dependency of Chile since 1888.

With a land area of 45 square miles (117 square km), Easter Island is 14 miles (23 km) long and 7 miles (11 km) wide. The island has a distinct triangular shape because it is formed by three extinct volcanoes.

Easter Island has a subtropical climate, and an average monthly temperature of 62° to 73° F (17° to 23° C). The island receives about 49 inches (125 cm) of rain each year. Rainfall occurs mainly in June and July, while September is the driest month. For most of the year, trade winds from the east and southeast sweep across the island. Few indigenous animals and plants are found on the island although yams, sweet potatoes, and sugarcane, all of which were introduced by settlers, abound.

THE HISTORY OF EASTER ISLAND

The original inhabitants of Easter Island were Polynesians, called the "long ears," who moved to the island before A.D. 500. After the Dutch first visited the island in 1722, a civil war raged. Slave raids from Peru, which began in 1862, and the spread of disease drastically reduced the number of inhabitants on the island. Toward the end of the nineteenth century, the population on Easter Island began to increase, and Chile annexed the island in 1888. The islanders became full Chilean citizens in 1965.

Left: Two youths from Easter Island wear their traditional clothing.

The Islanders

Approximately two thousand people live on Easter Island, the majority of whom are Polynesian. As a result, the island's culture is predominantly Polynesian despite a growing Chilean presence. Most of the island's population lives in Hanga-Roa, which is located on the western coast.

Moai

Easter Island is world famous for its mysterious giant stone statues, or moai. Built between A.D. 700 and 1600 by the island's early inhabitants, these enormous statues are widely believed to be representations of the islanders' sacred chiefs and gods. Carved from soft volcanic rock in the island's quarries, the statues range from 10 to 40 feet (3 to 12 m) in height. These were then placed on large stone platforms. Once erected, huge oval eye cavities and red tuff were added to the statues.

Today, more than six hundred moai are scattered throughout the island, and most can be found in Rapa Nui National Park. Covering 70 percent of the island, the park was declared a UNESCO World Heritage Site in 1995.

Above: The moai were erected on platforms, each of which could house up to fifteen statues. The largest standing moai is 37 feet (11 m) tall, while the largest unfinished one is 68 feet (21 m) tall.

ON THE MOVE

Theories regarding how early inhabitants transported the moai to their platforms vary. Local legends state that the moai walked from the quarry where they were carved to the platforms. Some archaeologists maintain the statues were lain on wooden sleds and moved to their final destination with log rollers.

Endangered Wildlife

The Southern Pudu

With a shoulder height of 14 to 18 inches (35 to 46 cm) and weighing approximately 13 to 30 pounds (6 to 13.5 kilograms), the southern pudu, or *Pudu pudu*, is the world's smallest deer. The animal has short, thick legs, a low-slung body, slender hooves, small and rounded ears, and small eyes. Male southern pudu grow spike antlers that eventually reach between 2 and 4 inches (5 and 10 cm) in length when they reach seven years. A female southern pudu usually has a single fawn that stays with its mother for eight to twelve months. Once it reaches adulthood, the southern pudu tends to live alone. Mainly active at dawn and dusk or during the night, the animal eats shrubs, leaves, bark, fruits, and berries.

Due to its physical build, the southern pudu can easily move through dense vegetation to escape predators. Its main predators include pumas, foxes, and dogs. When pursued, the southern pudu runs in a zigzag pattern and sometimes climbs trunks that lean over streams to escape the predator.

LOSS OF HABITATS

The destruction of the pudu's natural habitats through the clearing of land for logging and agriculture threatens the continued existence of the pudu species. In addition, the animal is hunted throughout its range. As a result, the pudus are listed as endangered species.

Left: **Two species of pudu exist in the world's humid and temperate forests. The southern pudu (*left*) lives in southern Chile and southwestern Argentina, while the northern pudu, or *Pudu mephistophiles*, can be spotted in the Andes of Colombia, Ecuador, and central Peru.**

The Andean Condor

Found at high elevations in the Andes Mountains, the Andean condor, or *Vultur gryphus*, is one of the largest flying land birds in the world. The bird, however, has been an endangered species since the 1970s.

The Andean condor has glossy black plumage with patches of white on its wings and a white ruff around its neck. Its head is featherless, and the male bird has a fleshy comb, or bump, on its forehead. Weighing 24 to 33 pounds (11 to 15 kg), the adult male Andean condor is heavier than its female counterpart. The bird can have a wingspan reaching 12 feet (3.7 m), allowing it to glide effortlessly for hundreds of miles (km). The Andean condor eats carrion, or dead flesh, although it has also been known to eat newborn or sick animals. The bird uses both its beak and feet to tear the flesh of its prey rather than kill it. With its excellent eyesight, the Andean condor is able to spot from the air prey that are miles (km) away.

Andean condors usually live in pairs. The female lays one egg every two years on open ground, on a ledge, or in a cave. Both the female and male bird look after the fledgling until it is ready to fend for itself about 180 days after it has hatched.

Above: The Andean condor has long played a significant role in the traditions of the Andes people. The condor is sometimes killed in religious rituals, and its feathers are used for decorative purposes. For the Andes people, killing an Andean condor also signals a young man's entrance to adulthood.

VULNERABLE

Farmers often shoot the Andean condor thinking that the bird kills livestock. Alternatively, they poison carrion that the bird eats to get rid of this unwanted pest. One other threat facing the Andean Condor is illegal poaching, since the bird is regarded as a highly prized catch.

Environmental Issues

Air pollution is one of the chief environmental problems in Chile, especially in the capital city. This has created a large hole in the ozone layer, which poses a threat to Chileans, especially those living in the south.

Causes of Santiago's Air Pollution

Industrial activity and emissions from automobiles are the major causes behind air pollution in Chile. Today, Santiago, with almost a million private vehicles in use, has the most severe air pollution in the country. Even though the city's emission level for pollutants is not drastically higher than in other cities, pollutants often become trapped around Santiago because it is situated in a valley between the coastal ranges and the Andes mountains.

Air pollution endangers the health of Santiago's residents, at times resulting in severe lung diseases. Many children and adults alike, suffer from asthma, a medical condition that causes breathing difficulties.

Left: **On certain days, a thick smog hovers over the sky in Santiago. The pollution problem in Santiago is worse during winter because wind and rainfall levels are at their lowest. Wind and rain help to reduce the pollutants in the air.**

58

Left: **Due to massive copper production, mining and smelting operations in Chile release a high level of pollutants into the air. In most cases, water is also polluted by industrial wastes from the factories.**

A Thinning Ozone Layer

The layer of ozone in the atmosphere protects Earth's surface from harmful ultraviolet rays. Excessive pollution reduces the ozone layer and sometimes creates a hole in this protective shield. Over the skies of southern Chile, as a result of global air pollution, is a gaping hole in the ozone layer. Ultraviolet rays can cause skin cancer, which can be fatal.

Close to Antarctica, the Chilean town of Punta Arenas is directly beneath the ozone hole. To avoid the potentially harmful rays, the residents of Punta Arenas are advised to stay indoors during the late mornings and early afternoons. When in the sun, residents wear protective clothing to avoid the ultraviolet rays.

Measures taken

The Chilean government is now trying to reduce the number of vehicles in Santiago. On July 5, 2002, during a severe smog, about twenty-five hundred factories were ordered to temporarily cease operation while more than a quarter of a million motorists had to stay off the roads in the capital. In 1998, in collaboration with the U.S. Department of Energy's Clean Cities program, Chile made plans to build a fleet of buses that run on natural gas. The government is also making efforts to relocate factories, in order to reduce the pollution in Santiago.

TRAINED AT A YOUNG AGE

From an early age, school children in Punta Arenas are taught ways to lower their risk of receiving the harmful ultraviolet rays that pass through the hole in the ozone layer. Before going out, they apply a generous amount of sunscreen, wear thick clothes that cover their arms and legs, and sport dark sunglasses.

The Mapuches

The Mapuches were the largest group of Araucanian Indians native to Chile and Argentina. Before the arrival of the Spaniards in 1541, almost two million Mapuche people inhabited the southern half of Chile and Argentina. Today, about 10 percent of the Chilean population identify themselves as Mapuches.

Three Hundred Years of Resistance

In the mid-1500s, Pedro de Valdivia and his men met with fierce native resistance when they tried to move southward from the Bío-Bío river into the area where the Araucanians lived. The Araucanians collectively organized their military against this potential foreign threat. Under the leadership of Lautaro, a Mapuche chief, the native inhabitants successfully defeated de Valdivia's forces in a 1553 battle, in which de Valdivia was killed. At one point, the powerful Araucanians came close to destroying the Spanish colony of Santiago. Territorial conflict did not cease for the next three centuries. In the early 1800s, when Spain lost its colonies in South America, newly-established Argentine and Chilean states began to take over the Araucanian territory. The displaced Araucanians were forced to stay in reservations.

Left: On August 5, 1998, Mapuches came out in full force to protest the construction of six hydroelectric dams in southern Chile. When built, the six dams will displace hundreds of Mapuche families.

Contemporary Mapuches

When the Mapuches were put in reservations, they farmed the land which they owned collectively. In the 1980s, however, the Chilean government gave land ownership to individuals in the reservations. Because the new land owners did not practice highly competitive methods of farming, they often incurred debt and eventually lost their land.

Today, the traditional Mapuche way of life is disappearing. Development, such as the construction of highways, threatens to displace the remaining Mapuche communities, and many of them have lost their ancestral homes. The present-day Mapuche has to move to other parts of the country in search of residence and work.

Nonetheless, international organizations consistently work to protect the rights of displaced Mapuches. Comite Exterior Mapuche (CEM) was set up in 1978 and replaced by the Mapuche International Link (MIL) in 1996. The MIL has departments that monitor issues, such as human rights and education, of Mapuches in Chile and other parts of the world.

Above: **Weaving is one of the skills that the Mapuches rely on for their livelihood.**

Pablo Neruda

Pablo Neruda (1904–73) was a Chilean poet and diplomat. Born Neftalí Ricardo Reyes Basoalto in Parral, Chile, Neruda spent his childhood and youth in Temuco, where he met Gabriela Mistral, another famous Chilean writer. Neruda started writing articles for newspapers at the age of thirteen, and adopted the pen name "Pablo Neruda" in 1920, when he wrote in the literary journal *Selva Austral*. He took the name Neruda from Czechoslovak poet Jan Neruda (1834–1891), who was an active promoter of Czech patriotism. Neruda's first collection of poems, *Crepusculario*, was published in Spanish in 1923. In the next year, Neruda published *Twenty Love Poems and a Song of Despair*.

Neruda's Political and Literary Career

Neruda took an early interest in politics. When he turned twenty-three, the Chilean government made him an honorary consul and sent him to various parts of the world, including Bueno Aires, Barcelona, Burma, and Java.

Below: **Pablo Neruda is one of the most widely-read Latin-American poets in the world.** *Twenty Love Poems and a Song of Despair* **has sold over a million copies since it was first published.**

Left: **In 1971, Neruda received the Nobel Prize for Literature.**

From the 1940s, many of Neruda's works reflected the political struggle of the socialists in South America. He is also known for his touching love poems, especially those from *One Hundred Love Sonnets* (1959). Some of them were dedicated to his wife Matilde Urrutia. Among his other books were *Residence on Earth* (1933), written in South Asia, and *Canto General* (1950), an epic work that chronicles South America's social history.

In 1945, Neruda joined the Communist Party in Chile and was elected senator. In 1947, he opposed President Gonzáles Videla's harsh treatment of strikers and trade unions and went into exile until 1952. Within these five years, Neruda lived with his wife Matilde in various parts of Europe and also on Chile's Isla Negra. There, he wrote *Memorial de Isla Negra*, a five-volume autobiography that was published on his sixtieth birthday. In 1950, Neruda received the International Peace Prize. He was also awarded the Stalin Prize and the Lenin Peace Prize in 1953.

From 1971 to 1972, at the time of Salvador Allende's Marxist regime, Neruda served as Chile's ambassador to France. When he was diagnosed with cancer in 1972, Neruda resigned. He passed away in Santiago on September 23, 1973.

Bernardo O'Higgins

Through dedication and perseverance, Bernardo O'Higgins helped win Chile's independence from Spain in 1817. He became the country's first head of state, or supreme director. Since then, he has been considered the founding father of Chile.

Believed to have been born on August 20, 1778, O'Higgins grew up in the southern Chilean town of Chillán. He was the son of Ambrosio O'Higgins, governor of Chile and later viceroy of Peru. After studying in Peru and Spain, O'Higgins traveled to London to continue his education. While in London, he came into contact with a group of political activists, all of whom were dedicated to the independence of Latin America. Through these associations, O'Higgins developed a deep sense of national pride in Chile.

Chile's path toward independence began in 1808, when France's Napoleon I invaded Spain. Concerned about its own defense, Spain left Chile and its other colonies uncontrolled. On September 18, 1810, a national junta was established in Santiago, and, by 1811, Chile had its own congress, of which O'Higgins was a member.

Left: **Bernardo O'Higgins secured Chile's independence in the 1817 battle against Spanish forces.**

Left: **A statue of Bernardo O'Higgins is located in the city of Coquimbo.**

In 1814, Peruvian-led forces invaded Chile to reestablish royal authority. During this time, O'Higgins rose through the military ranks to become general in chief of the opposition forces. After his defeat by royalist troops in October 1814, O'Higgins fled to Argentina. With the support of Argentine general José de San Martín, O'Higgins returned to Chile to defeat the Spanish in 1817.

Supreme Director

O'Higgins was elected supreme director in February 1817. As supreme director, he set about creating a new government, laid the grounds for peace and order, and built a strong navy. He also introduced economic and social reforms aimed at modernizing the newly founded independent state. These reforms, however, antagonized the Roman Catholic Church as well as Chilean aristocrats. The lack of widespread support for his policies led to his forced resignation in 1823. O'Higgins lived in exile in Peru until his death in 1842.

Popular Beverages

In Chile, festivities are often accompanied by traditional drinks. For instance, on Independence Day, a toast is never complete without *chicha* (CHEE-cha). The early chicha drinkers were the Incas from Peru, who used fermented corn and water. In Chile, chicha is a fermented fruit juice, and can be made from grapes, apples, or any other fruit.

Pisco

A popular beverage in Chile, pisco is consumed on special occasions as well as on a regular basis. Aside from Chileans, Peruvians also enjoy this drink. The alcohol used in pisco is distilled from white muscat grapes that are grown in the area around Valle del rio Elqui in central Chile and also in Pisco Peru. Chilean and Peruvian wine producers have a long history of disputes over which country originated the word "pisco."

CHICHA COCIDA

One type of chicha is *chicha cocida* (CHEE-chah ko-SEE-dah), which is fermented grape juice that has been boiled and then mixed with honey.

Below: **Cola is often added to pisco. One other way of drinking pisco, is to add freshly-squeezed lemon or lime juice to pisco. This concoction is called "pisco sour."**

A Christmas Drink

Another special drink is *cola de mono* (KOH-lah dee MAWH-noh), a milk punch that is traditionally consumed during the Christmas season. The name translates to mean "monkey's tail." Served chilled, cola de mono is a delightful mixture of coffee, milk, eggs, vanilla, and *aguardiente* (ah-gwah-dee-YAN-teh), or alcohol that is made from grain. A stick of cinnamon is sometimes added to give that extra flavor.

Chilean Wine

The best Chilean wines come from vineyards in the central valley. Grapevines thrive under the climate in this area, where seasons are defined and temperatures vary sharply between day and night. Because of its fine taste, Chilean wines are becoming very popular and are exported to countries such as Canada, the United States, Japan, and the United Kingdom.

Agüita

After meals, Chileans may enjoy a hot cup of *agüita* (ah-GWEE-tah). Traditionally consumed for its medicinal purposes, agüitas are herbal teas that are mixed with a wide variety of other herbs, such as basil, mint, and thyme. Citrus fruits such as lemons and oranges are also popular additions. The ingredients are steeped in hot water and sometimes sugar is added to sweeten the brew.

Valparaíso

Valparaíso is a city north of Santiago and is part of the Valparaíso region in Chile. Occupying an area of 6,193 square miles (15,900 square kilometers), Valparaíso is home to more than 290,000 residents. The city is 84 miles (135 km) from Santiago.

Birth of a City

In 1536, Spanish captain Juan de Saavedra anchored on the bay of Valparaíso to become the first Spaniard to visit the area. He named it Valparaíso, after his birthplace in Spain. However, the settlement was only fully established after Pedro de Valdivia arrived there in 1544.

Because of its strategic location, the city was a busy port during the sixteenth and the seventeenth centuries. Ships that headed for the Pacific islands passed Cape Horn and stopped at Valparaíso to refuel and replenish supplies. In the nineteenth century, many merchants came from England, Germany, and France to establish trade. The first bank in Chile was located in Valparaíso; the city also opened the first public library in South America.

Left: The city's rapid growth during the nineteenth century came to a halt when the Panama Canal opened in 1914 and ships started to use the Canal instead of sailing around South America.

Left: **The elaborate system of funicular elevators is a unique feature in Valparaíso.**

A Fascinating Tourist Spot

The city of Valparaíso sits on steep cliffs overlooking the picturesque bay. A unique system of transportation that consists of funicular elevators, or cable railways, brings the city's residents around the steep cliffs. From the banks and shops at the lower part of the city to the slums at its top, fifteen funicular elevators link the different parts of the city.

Some of the significant places in Valparaíso are the National Congress building, the Naval and Maritime Museum, and the Municipal Theater. Previously situated in Santiago, the National Congress building in Valparaíso was opened by Pinochet in 1990.

A Gabriela Mistral Museum House was dedicated by the city to the outstanding writer in memory of her literary achievements. Chilean poet Pablo Neruda also had a house in Valparaíso, which is now a museum that exhibits some of his personal belongings.

Today, Valparaíso is the largest seaport in South America and the terminal of the Transandine Railway. The city manufactures textiles, leather goods, paint, and chemicals.

MILD WEATHER

The average temperature in Valparaíso during the summer is 68° F (20° C), and 59° F (15° C) during winter. The mild weather is a major attraction for tourists, aside from the city's old-world charm.

War of the Pacific

By the mid-1800s, Chile was in debt because of its outstanding loans and costly imports. To clear its debts, the government turned to the valuable minerals in the Atacama Desert. Bolivia, however, also staked a claim to this area. In 1866 and 1874, the two states signed treaties that allowed both countries to mine the desert between the 23rd and 24th parallel south latitude without taxes imposed by either country. In 1879, Bolivia raised the taxes of Chilean mining companies in Tarapacá and Antofagasta and also tried to monopolize the mining industry with neighboring country Peru. This led to the War of the Pacific (1879–1883).

Battles and Occupation

Chilean forces occupied the city of Antofagasta in 1879, which led to a declaration of war from Bolivia. Assisted by its ally, Peru, the Bolivian troops faced the Chilean navy in February 1879. Because of its well-organized navy, Chile emerged victorious from naval battles in the Bolivian coastal region.

Left: **The wealth of minerals in the Atacama Desert was the chief dispute between Chile and the neighboring countries of Peru and Bolivia in the nineteenth century.**

Chile then occupied the capital of Peru, Lima, on January 17, 1881. This marked the beginning of Chile's ten-year occupation in Lima. In 1883, Peru and Chile came together to sign the Treaty of Ancón. The Peruvian province of Tarapacá and the Bolivian province of Antofagasta were ceded to Chile. In addition, the Chileans gained control of the nitrate exports. Victory over its neighbors gave Chile the new status of a superpower, both in terms of its military and its economy.

Above: The Esmeralda had its last voyages during the War of the Pacific, when the warship and its captain went down in the history of Chile's naval victories.

The Esmeralda

When the War of the Pacific began, the Chilean navy only had eight ships. The oldest was *The Esmeralda*, a wooden warship. At Iquique, Chilean captain Arturo Prat Chacón commanded the *Esmeralda*, and met two Peruvian warships. An intense battle began. *The Esmeralda* was outnumbered, but Prat and his crew continued to fend off the attacks. At one point, Prat fearlessly boarded one of the enemies' ships. He suffered two fatal bullet wounds and died, but the battle continued as the Chilean crew refused to surrender. After more than three hours of relentless fighting, *The Esmeralda* finally sank. The bravery of the captain and his crew is honored every year on the May 21 anniversary.

MOVING SOUTH

After its military victory over Bolivia and Peru, Chilean forces fought the Araucanians who lived in the south. 1882 marked the year when the Araucanians, mainly Mapuches, were defeated. The native inhabitants moved on to reservations in 1884.

The Women of Chile

For centuries, Chilean women were given little recognition for their contributions to society. The women's rights movement in Chile progressed during the twentieth century, and women today play an active role in all aspects of Chilean life.

Traditionally, women were expected to stay home, raise children, and take care of the household. By the early twentieth century, however, women had began to venture out of the home and into the workforce. The important role that Chilean women played in society was finally acknowledged in 1949 when women gained full rights to vote. During the 1960s and 1970s, women's rights movements veered in a new direction as women became more politically active. Following the 1973 coup, many women organized groups that campaigned strongly against human rights abuses. In addition, more women entered the workforce because many men had been fired from their jobs, were exiled, were jailed, or simply disappeared after trying to organize political groups that opposed Pinochet's government.

WOMEN IN THE WORKFORCE

In 1910, Chile had 3,980 female teachers, but only three female lawyers. Two decades later, the female enrollment at the University of Chile's law school rose to 124. About 38 percent of the students in the dental school were also female.

Below: Women continue to play the role of main care-giver in Chilean families, although many have joined the workforce.

Women in Contemporary Chile

Following Chile's return to democracy at the start of the 1990s, the government established the National Women's Service, or SERNAM. This organization is responsible for ensuring equal rights for women through policies and laws, encouraging more women to join the workforce, and improving their quality of life. Women also continue to be politically active and aware. Three female ministers and two female senators serve in the current government, the highest number of women ever chosen to do so.

Today, more women are working in professions that were traditionally male-oriented, such as law and medicine. While Chilean women make up about one-third of the workforce in Chile, they remain underrepresented in senior business positions. Women also continue to earn less than their male counterparts. On average, a woman's income is barely two-thirds that of a man when they both hold the same job.

Although Chilean women have made great progress, they continue to press for further changes. These changes include the passage of laws that will protect them against pressing social problems, such as domestic violence, poverty, and discrimination.

Above: **Women in Chile are increasingly adopting professions that were previously dominated by men. These two marine biologists study the aquatic life off the coast of Chile.**

74

RELATIONS WITH NORTH AMERICA

Chilean-U.S. relations date back to the early nineteenth century. Since then, mutual interests between North America and Chile have risen dramatically. Trade links began in the 1830s, and Chilean emigration to the United States started in 1848 when gold discoveries first drew Chileans to California. North American relations with Chile were not so warm during the final years of General Augusto Pinochet's dictatorship as both the United States and Canada called for the return of democracy in Chile.

Opposite: **Familiar advertisements for American companies, such as the fast food chain MacDonald's, are a common sight on the streets of Chile.**

Today, Chile, the United States, and Canada enjoy strong relations. All three countries are working hard to develop and solidify their economic, political, social, and academic ties. In addition, both the United States and Canada continue to be Chile's main trading partners and investors.

Both the United States and Canada are home to a significant number of citizens of Chilean descent. While some Chilean-North Americans have lived in North America for generations, they still take pride in their heritage, and they have established numerous organizations that pay homage to their native homeland.

Above: **Chairman and CEO of NASDAQ International John Hilley (*right*) gives Chilean president Ricardo Lagos (*left*) a tour of the NASDAQ Stock Market during the president's visit to New York in November 2000.**

Historical Relations

The United States and Chile first established diplomatic relations on January 27, 1823, during the administrations of U.S. president James Monroe and Chilean supreme director Bernardo O'Higgins. Joaquín Campino led the first Chilean mission to the United States in 1827. While in the United States, Campino negotiated a trade agreement between the two nations. The treaty was signed in 1832 and opened the way for trading links between the two countries.

Tensions arose between the United States and Chile during the War of the Pacific between 1879 and 1883. The United States feared Chilean dominance in the South Pacific might lead to European intervention in the conflict, and attempted to act as mediator between the warring nations of Chile, Bolivia, and Peru. The U.S. government's attempt to avoid territorial losses for Peru, however, caused widespread anti-American feeling in Chile until the fighting ended in 1883.

Chile declared its neutrality during the two World Wars. After the end of World War II in 1945, Chile, the United States, and Canada all joined the United Nations (U.N.). At this time, bilateral discussions between the United States and Chile focused mainly on U.S. trade investments in Chile, the price of copper, and security issues in South America. Relations between the United States and Chile gradually worsened during the 1960s.

Left: **President Lagos addresses the General Assembly of the United Nations at the Millenium Summit in New York in September 2000.**

Left: **Canadian Prime Minister Jean Chretien (*left*) is greeted by former Chilean president Eduardo Frei (*right*) during Chretien's 1995 tour of Latin America.**

Following the election of Salvador Allende as Chile's president in 1970, the United States worked to undermine the socialist government and supported the 1973 military coup that brought General Augusto Pinochet to power. Anxious to protect major Canadian investments in Chile, the Canadian government quickly joined the United States as one of the first countries to recognize General Pinochet's regime.

The U.S. position toward Chile changed in the mid-1970s. When Chile's opposition leader and former foreign minister Orlando Letelier was assassinated on the streets of Washington, D.C., the U.S. government worked to find the guilty parties. The Chilean government failed to hand over officers accused of being involved in the assassination, and this resulted in U.S. sanctions against Chile. From late 1970s, under the Carter administration which strongly emphasized human rights, to the late 1980s, the United States stepped up its criticisms of the Pinochet regime's human rights abuses and called for Chile's return to democracy.

Both Canada and the United States welcomed the restoration of democracy in Chile by 1990. Diplomatic relations between Chile and North America reached a high point in the 1990s during Chilean president Eduardo Frei's time in office. The three nations worked to strengthen and expand ties.

STATE VISITS

Recent state visits between the three nations have helped forge closer ties. In February 1997, Chilean president Eduardo Frei Montalva visited U.S. president Bill Clinton in Washington, D.C. One year later, President Bill Clinton went on a two-day state visit to Chile. In May 2001, Adrienne Clarkson, governor general of Canada, met Chilean president Ricardo Lagos during a six-day state visit to Chile.

Current Relations

Relations between Chile and the United States and Canada today are strong. All three countries work closely together in areas such as democracy and human rights, defense, global security, and trade and investment.

Trade ties between the three nations have strengthened over recent years. The United States is Chile's single-largest trading partner and its most important foreign investor. At present, the Chilean and U.S. governments are negotiating a free trade agreement that will eventually lead to Chile's membership in the North American Free Trade Agreement (NAFTA). In 1997, Chile and Canada signed the Canada-Chile Free Trade Agreement (CCFTA). Since then, bilateral trade between the two countries has increased greatly. Canada has invested $U.S. 11.6 billion in existing and planned investments in Chile in sectors such as mining, forestry, telecommunications, financial services, and energy. This makes Chile the largest recipient of Canadian investment in Latin America and Canada the second-largest investor in Chile. Canada and Chile also signed the Canada-Chile Agreement on Environmental Cooperation (CCAEC) in 1997, in which the two nations agreed to improve environmental cooperation and enforce environmental laws related to water, air, toxic substances, and wildlife.

Left: U.S. president George W. Bush (*left*) is congratulated by Canadian Prime Minister Jean Chretien (*center*) as Chilean president Ricardo Lagos (*right*) looks on. Both Chile and the United States signed an agreement that will implement on the American continent the world's largest free trade zone by the end of 2005. The agreement was signed in Quebec City, Canada in 2001.

Left: U.S. actress Mia Farrow talks to a young patient at a cerebral palsy rehabilitation center in Santiago in March 1998. Farrow arrived in Chile in support of Chile's Alter Ego Foundation, which aids children who have neurological problems.

Humanitarian Ties

Chile, the United States, and Canada are members of various organizations, such as the U.N., the World Health Organization (WHO), and UNESCO, that work to improve the lives of people around the world. Chilean, U.S., and Canadian troops have served together with various U.N. peacekeeping force missions and are currently serving side by side in Bosnia and Herzegovina.

North American Aid

The Canadian International Development Agency (CIDA) is currently working in Chile. The organization focuses on industrial, environmental, educational, social assistance, and health programs. CIDA also provides funding for Canadian institutions, associations, and nongovernmental organizations (NGOs) based in Chile. Some of these NGOs include the World Bank, the United Nations Development Programme, and the United Nations Children's Fund (UNICEF).

Aside from the aid agencies, private companies in North America have helped Chile in times of need. U.S.-based Philip Morris Companies Inc. has a Humanitarian Aid Program that assists international relief efforts. In 1960, when Chile was struck by an earthquake, Philip Morris helped victims by way of a large donation to the Red Cross in Chile.

Immigration

The first wave of Chilean emigration to the United States occurred in 1848 during the gold rush in California. Ships sailing from San Francisco to East Coast ports via Cape Horn stopped at Valparaíso and other South American cities during the journey. Sailors and passengers told the residents about the discovery, and news about the gold rush spread quickly. Many of the early Chilean immigrants were experienced miners who settled in California in the hope of striking it rich.

More than a century later, during the 1960s, some Chilean professionals, such as doctors, educators, and engineers, moved to the United States in search of a better life. The second main wave of immigrants, however, began to arrive in the United States following the establishment of General Pinochet's military dictatorship in Chile in 1973. Most of those who fled Chile feared political persecution. A number of Chileans who had taken up residence in the United States returned to their homeland when General Pinochet stepped down from power and moves were made to return Chile to a democratic nation by 1990. Those who remained mainly lived in New York and California.

Emigration to Canada began in 1970 following the election of socialist Salvador Allende as Chile's president. The second and much larger wave of Chilean immigrants arrived in Canada after the 1973 military coup that brought General Pinochet to power. While many Chileans were forced to leave their country by the military government because of their political beliefs, others fled because of infringements on their basic human rights.

Chilean immigrants settled throughout Canada, particularly in the country's urban and industrial centers. During the 1970s, the favorable economies in Alberta and Manitoba attracted many Chileans to these areas, while those arriving in the 1980s chose to settle in Ontario and British Columbia. As in the United States, these immigrants were well-educated and trained in engineering, manufacturing, and the construction and transportation sectors, as well as in health care, the arts, and sports.

A Proactive Community

Chilean immigrants who made the journey to North America continued to take an interest in their homeland. Many Chileans sent money and food to family members and friends in Chile, while others worked for Chile's transition to democracy until the end of the military regime in the late 1980s.

Left: **Former Chilean president Salvador Allende (*left*) went to the United States on an official visit in 1972.**

Chileans in North America

Today, about sixty-nine thousand Chileans live in the United States, mainly in New York and California. More than thirty-three thousand Chileans have settled in Canada, and vibrant communities can be found in Quebec, Ontario, Alberta, and British Columbia. Nearly every city with a sizable Chilean population has restaurants, bakeries, and shops selling Chilean foods and goods.

North America's Chilean community plays an active role in promoting a number of Spanish language magazines and newspapers and creating a variety of societies for women, politics, as well as finance and social welfare.

Chilean-North Americans have set up the Chilean American Foundation (CAF), a nonprofit, nonpolitical organization that is based in Washington, D.C. The CAF was founded in 1990 to provide financial support for small social projects in Chile aimed at helping Chilean children and youths.

With its main office in Vancouver, the Institute for the Americas is an organization that fosters social, economic, and cultural ties between Canada and the countries of Latin America, including Chile. The organization also promotes professional development through educational programs, such as courses teaching the Spanish language, and cultural exchanges within the continent.

Left: **A priest delivers a speech at the U.S. embassy in Santiago during a memorial service for victims of the September 11 World Trade Center attack in New York. Special attention was also given to Chileans who were killed in the attack.**

Left: **Canadian attacker Terry Dunfiel (*right*) from the Canadian Sub-20 Team dribbles the ball away from Chilean player Jaime Valdes (*left*) in a friendly match in Santiago. This match is an opportunity for North Americans living in Chile to support their home teams when working or studying in Chile.**

North Americans in Chile

A small number of North Americans make their homes in Chile, twelve thousand of whom are Americans living predominantly in the areas surrounding Santiago. Many North American visitors to the country are of Chilean descent, and they often return to their native homeland to visit family and friends or learn more about their ancestry. In addition to hereditary ties, tourism is another reason why North Americans travel and stay in Chile. About 120,000 Americans visit the country each year.

The United States and Canada both have embassies in Santiago. In addition, both a Chilean Canadian and a Chilean American Chamber of Commerce operate in Chile. These chambers serve the Chilean-North American business communities and enhance business ties and trade between Chile and North America.

Left: In October 1998, former Chilean president Patricio Aylwin received the J. William Fulbright prize for International Understanding for his efforts in bringing democracy and justice to Chile. The Fulbright Program aims to foster mutual understanding among nations through educational and cultural exchanges.

Academic Ties

The United States ranks first and Canada fifth as the most popular destinations for Chilean students wishing to pursue their studies overseas. Many Chilean universities and vocational schools also have exchange programs in North America.

Chile, Canada, and the United States take part in a number of educational exchanges and programs. In collaboration with the International Council for Canadian Studies (ICCS), the Chilean government, through the Chilean International Cooperation Agency (AGCI), set up the Foreign Government Awards (FGA) Program, which offers two scholarships to Canadians who want to do postgraduate study or research in Chile. Established in 1996, seven Chilean and Canadian business schools promote bilateral academic exchanges between Chilean and Canadian institutions in the areas of financing and business research, among others.

Chile also participates in the Fulbright Program, which was established by the U.S. Congress in 1946.

THE CANADIAN EDUCATION CENTER

To meet the growing demands of students wishing to study in Canada, a Canadian Education Center was set up in Santiago. Founded in 1998, the main aim of the center is to help Canadian educational institutions promote their courses, programs, and products in Chile, as well assist Chileans interested in pursuing their studies in Canada.

Famous Chileans in North America

Born in 1942, Chilean Isabel Allende is an internationally acclaimed author whose works have been translated into more than twenty-seven languages. Allende worked as a journalist in print, on television, and in movie documentaries before moving to Venezuela in 1975 with her husband and family. She wrote her first novel *The House of the Spirits* in 1982, which was then made into a Hollywood movie in 1994, starring Winona Ryder, Meryl Streep, and Glenn Close. After divorcing her husband in 1987, Allende married American Willie Gordon in 1988 and has since lived in California. Allende continues to write novels and does extensive book tours throughout the United States and Europe. She has also taught literature at universities in Virginia, New Jersey, and California.

Actor Cristiãn de la Fuente is Chilean. A well-loved leading man in Chile, de la Fuente has also gained popularity in the United States since starring in the popular CBS drama series *Family Law*. He has taken his talent to the big screen and has starred opposite Sylvester Stallone in *Driven* (2001) and Jon Bon Jovi in John Carpenter's *Vampires: Los Muertos* (2001).

Below: **Chilean actor Cristiãn de la Fuente (*third from left*) poses with the cast of the 2001 film *Driven*, which is directed by Renny Harlin (*second from right*) and also stars Sylvester Stallone (*second from left*).**

A B C D

N

PERU

BOLIVIA

1

Putre
Arica
TARAPACÁ
Tarapacá
Iquique La Tirana

BRAZIL

ANTOFAGASTA

Chuquicamata El Tatio Geyser

Tropic of Capricorn Antofagasta Valle de la Luna

PARAGUAY

Escondida
Cerro Chajnantor

Cerro Paranal

ATACAMA Nevada Ojos del Salado
(22,614 ft/6,893 m)

2

*Rapa Nui
National Park*

Hanga-Roa

EASTER ISLAND

Valle de río Elqui

La Serena Las Campanas
Coquimbo Cerro Tololo

COQUIMBO

Viña del Mar **VALPARAÍSO**

*Juan Fernández
Islands* Valparaíso Isla Negra

SANTIAGO

PACIFIC Pomaire **REGION METROPOLITANA (SANTIAGO)** **URUGUAY**

Rancagua **LIBERTADOR GENERAL BERNARDO O'HIGGINS**

MAULE Linares
Parral

OCEAN **BÍO-BÍO** **ARGENTINA**

3 Concepción Chillán

Bío-Bío

Temuco

LA ARAUCANIA Villarrica

Valdivia *Ranco Lake*

Puerto Montt *Llanquihue Lake*

Chacao Straits **ATLANTIC**

Ancud Achao

Chiloé Island **LOS LAGOS** **OCEAN**

4

	National Boundary
	Regional Boundary
■	Capital
●	City
~	River

AISEN DEL GENERAL CARLOS IBANEZ DEL CAMPO

PATAGONIA

MAGELLANES Y DE LA ANTARCTICA CHILENA

5

*Torres del
Paine* Strait of Magellan

CHILE

Punta Arenas *Tierra del
Fuego*

Cape Horn

Achao B4
Aisen del General Carlos
    Ibanez del Campo
    (region) B4–B5
Ancud B4
Andes C1-B3
Antofagasta (city) B1
Antofagasta (region)
    B1–C2
Argentina B5–D2
Arica B1
Atacama (region) B1–C2
Atacama Desert B1–B2
Atlantic Ocean C5–D2

Bío-Bío (region) B3
Bío-Bío (river) B3
Bolivia B1–D1
Brazil D1–D3

Cape Horn C5
Cerro Chajnantor B1
Cerro Paranal B2
Cerro Tololo B2
Chacao Straits B4
Chillán B3
Chiloé Island B4
Concepción B3
Coquimbo (city) B2
Coquimbo (region) B2
Chuquicamata B1

Easter Island A2
El Tatio Geyser B1–C1
Escondida B1

Hanga-Roa A2

Iquique B1
Isla Negra B3

Juan Fernández Islands
    A3

La Araucania (region) B3
La Serena B2
La Tirana B1
Las Campanas B2
Lao (river) B1–C1
Libertador General
    Bernardo O'Higgins
    (region) B3
Linares B3
Llanquihue Lake B4

Above: Chile's central valley is an ideal region for vineyards.

Los Lagos (region)
    B3–B4

Magellanes y de la
    Antartica Chilena
    (region) B4–C5
Maule (region) B3

Nevado Ojas del Salado
    B2–C2

Pacific Ocean A1–B5
Paraguay C1–D2
Parral B3
Patagonia (Chile and
    Argentina) B4–B5
Peru B1
Pomaire B3
Puerto Montt B4
Punta Arenas B5
Putre B1

Rancagua B3

Ranco Lake B3
Rapa Nui National Park
    A2

Region Metropolitana
    (Santiago) (region)
    B3

Santiago (capital) B3
Strait of Magellan B5–C5

Tarapacá (city) B1
Tarapacá (region) B1–C1
Temuco B3
Tierra del Fuego
    (Chile and Argentina)
    B5–C5

Torres del Paine B5

Uruguay D2–D3

Valdivia B3
Valle de la Luna B1–C2
Valle de rio Elqui B2
Villarrica B3
Valparaíso (city) B3
Valparaiso (region) B2-
    B3
Viña del Mar B3

CHILE

How Is Your Geography?

Learning to identify the main geographical areas and points of a country can be challenging. Although it may seem difficult at first to memorize the locations and spellings of major cities or the names of mountain ranges, rivers, deserts, lakes, and other prominent physical features, the end result of this effort can be very rewarding. Places you previously did not know existed will suddenly come to life when referred to in world news, whether in newspapers, television reports, other books and reference sources, or on the Internet. This knowledge will make you feel a bit closer to the rest of the world, with its fascinating variety of cultures and physical geography.

Used in a classroom setting, the instructor can make duplicates of this map using a copy machine. (PLEASE DO NOT WRITE IN THIS BOOK!) Students can then fill in any requested information on their individual map copies. Used one-on-one, the student can also make copies of the map on a copy machine and use them as a study tool. The student can practice identifying place names and geographical features on his or her own.

Above: **Arica is one of the northernmost cities in Chile and closer to Peru and Bolivia than Chile's capital.**

Chile at a Glance

Official Name	Republic of Chile
Capital	Santiago
Official Language	Spanish
Population	15,328,467 (as of 2001)
Land Area	292,182 square miles (756,751 square km)
Administrative Regions	Aisen del General Carlos Ibanez del Campo, Antofagasta, La Araucania, Atacama, Bío-Bío, Coquimbo, El Libertador General Bernardo O'Higgins, Los Lagos, Magellanes y de la Antartica Chilena, Maule, Region Metropolitana (Santiago), Tarapacá, Valparaiso
Border Countries	Argentina, Bolivia, Peru
Highest Point	Nevado Ojos del Salado 22,614 feet (6,893 m)
Major Rivers	Bío-Bío, Loa, Valdivia
Main Religions	Roman Catholicism, Protestantism
Major Cities	Concepción, Santiago, Valparaíso, Viña del Mar
Major Holidays	Semana Santa (late March or early April)
	La Tirana (July 12–July 15)
	National Unity day (first Monday of September)
	Independence Day (September 18)
Major Exports	Chemicals, copper, fish, and fruits
Major Imports	Chemicals, consumer goods, electrical machinery, food, fuels, heavy industrial machinery, motor vehicles
Currency	Chilean peso (669 CLP =U.S. $1 as of 2002)

Opposite: **The stunning view from the coast of Easter Island attracts tourists from around the world.**

Glossary

Spanish Vocabulary

alfajor (ehl-fah-HOHR): desert consisting of layers of caramelized milk and thin pastry rolled in sugar.

aguardiente (ah-ghwah-dee-YAN-teh): grain alcohol.

agüita (ah-GWEE-tah): herbal tea.

asados (ah-SAH-dohs): barbecues.

bombo (BOHM-boh): a percussion instrument used in South America since pre-Colombian times.

cazuela (kah-SWEH-lah): soup that contains rice, potato and corn on a cob.

chicha cocida (CHEE-chah ko-SEE-dah): fermented grape juice that has been boiled and mixed with honey.

chueca (CHWEH-kah): a sport that resembles hockey and is played by the Mapuches.

cueca (KWEHY-kah): the national dance of Chile.

desayuno (deh-sah-JOO-noh): breakfast.

El Almuerzo (ehl ahl-moo-EHR-soh): lunch.

EL completo (ehl kohm-PLEH-toh): Chilean-style hotdog.

empanadas (ehm-pa-NAH-dahs): baked turnovers that are filled with chopped beef, cheese, or seafood.

ensalada chilena (ehn-sah-LAH-dah chee-LEH-nah): salad consisting of sliced tomatoes and onions, with oil, vinegar and cilantro dressing.

fútbol (foot-BOL): soccer.

guitarron (gee-tah-ROHN): a large bass guitar used in Chilean folk music.

huasos (WAH-sohs): Chilean cowboys.

humita (oo-MEE-tah): a mixture of mashed corn, fried onions, and basil that is wrapped in corn husks.

La comida (lah ko-MEE-dah): supper.

moai (moh-AH-ee): giant stone statues that were constructed centuries ago by Polynesians living on Easter Island.

once (OHN-say): late afternoon tea.

pastel de choclo (pah-STEHL dee CHOH-klo): corn casserole consisting of meat, vegetables, olives, and layers of corn.

pisco (PIS-koh): a liquor made from muscat grapes.

rayuela (rah-yoo-EH-lah): a traditional game that originated in Spain.

English Vocabulary

abdicate: to give up a high position.

annexed: incorporated into the domain of a city, country, or state.

annulled: invalidated or made void.

anthropologists: scientists who study the physical development and cultural customs of humans.

appointee: a person who is legally assigned to a position or task.

arable: suitable for farming.

archaeologists: scientists who study cultures or early peoples by examining their remains and artifacts.

arid: extremely dry or parched.

aristocrats: people who come from a line of nobles or are of a privileged class.

artifacts: handmade objects that belonged to an earlier time.

astronomy: the study of the physical universe beyond Earth's atmosphere.

breadwinners: persons who earn money and support family members or other people around them.

concoction: a mixture of ingredients.

democracy: a system of government where the supreme power is held by the people, who select representatives through elections.

designation: to officially name.

dictatorship: absolute power or control.

discrimination: action that is against a person or a group of people.

equator: the circle of the Earth that has the same distance from the North Pole and South Pole.

erupted: broken out in a sudden and violent manner.

extinct: no longer active or living.

flanked: placed or posted at the side of.

funicular elevators: cable cars that carry riders up and down steep hills.

geysers: hot springs that intermittently send up fountainlike jets of water and steam into the air.

impunity: exemption from punishment.

inauguration: the formal ceremony where a person assumes public office.

indigenous: originating in or characteristic of a particular region or country.

inflation: the rise in the prices of all goods and services.

infrastructure: the basic system of communications and transportation in an area.

introspective: examining a person's own mental and emotional states.

manganese: a hard, brittle, grayish white, metallic element.

maritime: referring to the sea.

Marxist: the system of thought developed by German philosopher Karl Marx, which focuses on the problems of class struggles.

mestizos: persons who are of American Indian and European descent.

mobility: the movement of people or individuals from place to place.

mythologize: to construct a legend.

oases: fertile areas in a desert region.

pensions: fixed allowances that are paid at regular intervals.

picturesque: beautiful.

plateau: a raised land area that has a relatively level surface.

precipitation: the amount of rain, hail, snow, or the like that has fallen at a place within a given period.

predators: animals that prey on and kill other animals, usually for food.

priorities: pressing matters that are given special attention.

quaint: having an old-fashioned charm.

regime: a system of rule or government.

sediments: minerals that are deposited by water, air, or ice.

summits: the highest part of a mountain or hill.

temperate: moderate in respect to temperature; not subject to prolonged extremes of hot or cold weather.

More Books to Read

Argentina, Chile, Paraguay, Uruguay. Country Fact File series. Anna Selby
   (Raintree/Steck-Vaughn)

Chile. Cultures of the World series. Jane Kohen Winter (Marshall Cavendish)

Chile. Enchantment of the World series. Sylvia McNair (Children's Press)

Chile: Land of Poets and Patriots. Irene Flum Galvin (Silver Burditt Press)

Chile: Major World Nations series. Christopher Dwyer (Chelsea House)

Chile in Pictures. Visual Geography series. Nathan A. Haverstock (Lerner)

Folk Tales from Chile. Library of Folklore series. Brenda Hughes (Hippocrene Books)

Rediscovering Easter Island: How History Is Invented. How History is Invented series.
   Kathy Pelta (Lerner)

Videos

Easter Island. Secrets of the Lost Empire II series. (NOVA)

Full Circle with Michael Palin: Chile/Bolivia and Peru. (PBS Home Video)

The Oldest Mummies in the World. Mummies and Pyramids: Egypt and Beyond series.
   (World Almanac)

Pablo Neruda. The Hispanic and Latin American Heritage Video Collection series.
   (Schlessinger)

Web Sites

www.chile-usa.org/

www.mapuche-nation.org/english/frontpage.htm

www.islandheritage.org

www.visit-chile.org

Due to the dynamic nature of the Internet, some web sites stay current longer than others. To find additional web sites, use a reliable search engine with one or more of the following keywords to help you locate information about Chile. Keywords: *Isabel Allende, Atacama, cueca, Easter Island, Bernardo O'Higgins, moai, Santiago.*

Index